CONTENTS

Note	2
Acknowledgements	2
Glossary	2
Brief Background	2
OPOR HOREV	2
Day 0: 22 December 1948	4
Day 1: 23 December 1948	6
Day 2: 24 December 1948	8
Day 3: 25 December 1948	11
Day 4: 26 December 1948	13
Day 5: 27 December 1948	20
Day 6: 28 December 1948	22
Day 7: 29 December 1948	29
Day 8: 30 December 1948	36
Day 9: 31 December 1948	41
Day 10: 1 January 1949	46
Day 11: 2 January 1949	49
Day 12: 3 January 1949	52
Day 13: 4 January 1949	56
Day 14: 5 January 1949	59
Day 15: 6 January 1949	64
Day 16: 7 January 1949	66
Ceasefire	69
End of OPOR HOREV	71

Helion & Company Limited
26 Willow Road, Solihull, West Midlands, B91 1UE, England
Tel. 0121 705 3393
Fax 0121 711 4075

Email: info@helion.co.uk   Website: www.helion.co.uk   Twitter: @helionbooks   Visit our blog http://blog.helion.co.uk/

Published by Helion & Company 2015
Designed and typeset by Kerrin Cocks, SA Publishing Services
Cover designed by Kerrin Cocks, SA Publishing Services
Printed by Henry Ling Ltd, Dorchester, Dorset

Text © Shlomo Aloni 2015
Monochrome images sourced by the author
Colour profiles drawn and commentary written by Tom Cooper, © Tom Cooper 2015
Maps drawn by George Anderson © Helion & Company Limited 2015

Every reasonable effort has been made to trace copyright holders and to obtain their permission for the use of copyright material. The author and publisher apologize for any errors or omissions in this work, and would be grateful if notified of any corrections that should be incorporated in future reprints or editions of this book.

Cover: The ILAF inventory included eight T-6s, but 1108 did not fly during HOREV and 1103 did not fly attack missions during HOREV, so the actual maximum T-6 force was six aircraft, as flown during the Day 5 afternoon mission to raid Manshiya. Colour profile - The Avia S.199 'D-121' did not follow the trend of ever-larger serials, but – contrary to its looks during the summer of 1948 – did receive full markings of the No. 101 'First Fighter' Squadron, including its spinner in red, and red and white stripes on the rudder. Notable is that the serial was applied in black and blue colors, and that the 'Red Cross' insignia over the first-aid package was replaced with the Star of David applied in red.

ISBN 978-1-910294-11-6

British Library Cataloguing-in-Publication Data.
A catalogue record for this book is available from the British Library.
All rights reserved. No part of this publication may be reproduced, stored in a retrieval system, or transmitted, in any form, or by any means, electronic, mechanical, photocopying, recording or otherwise, without the express written consent of Helion & Company Limited.
For details of other military history titles published by Helion & Company
Limited contact the above address, or visit our website: http://www.helion.co.uk.
We always welcome receiving book proposals from prospective authors.

Note

One of the most important virtues of an officer is credibility. A military organization supposedly cannot win a war without credibility along the chain of command. It is therefore assumed that most - surely not all - of the debriefs quoted in this presentation are credible; latter accounts from biographies, interviews and memoirs are therefore mostly ignored in this presentation of ILAF operations during Operation HOREV. Largely, this book is not a narrative, a story or a tale but a plain presentation of ILAF operations, mostly from an Israeli perspective, along the timeline of HOREV. It is not fully complete; it is not absolutely accurate; it is certainly concise and perhaps precise; but it is the best possible effort at this point in time.
Shlomo Aloni
1 November 2013

Acknowledgements

This presentation of ILAF operations during ILDF Operation HOREV benefits from materials that have been gathered over a timeframe of more than 20 years from national archives and personal collections. The author thanks Oded Abarbanell, Haggai Agmon, Daniel Arber, Rudy Augarten, Zvi Avidror, Israel Ben-Shachar, Yeshayahu Bodilewsky, Judah Borovik, Jules Cuburnek, Brian Cull, Yoav Efrati, Eli Eyal, Ron Feldman, Seymour Feldman, Michel Finegood, Aaron Finkel, Leon Frankel, Shaya Gazit, Udi Gazit, Josef Gideoni, Johnny Harris, Leif Hellstrom, Moti Hod, Arie Jacoby, Eddy Kaplansky, Shabtai Katz, Josef Keidar, Samuel Laron, Lou Lenart, Zvi Lavon, George Lichter, Gideon Lichtman, Hugo Marom, Ariel Naor, Nathan Navot, David Nicolle, Josef Ofer, Benjamin Peled, Moshe Peled, Yoram Peled, Asher Roth, Meir Ruff, Boris Senior, Daniel Shapira, Smoky Simon, Pessach Tal, Yoash Tsiddon, Ran Yahalom and Zahik Yavneh, as well as ILDA, ILPO and UKNA for documents, memories and photos. All presented photos originated from collections of the aforementioned.

Glossary

AAA	Anti-Aircraft Artillery
AMU	Air Maintenance Unit
CASEVAC	Casualty Evacuation
EGAF	Egypt Air Force
EGDF	Egypt Defense Force (armed forces/army)
EGNF	Egypt Naval Force (Navy)
FRUS	Foreign Relations of the United States, a publication that constitutes the official record of the foreign policy of USA
GMT	Greenwich Mean Time
HQ	Headquarters
ILAF	Israel Air Force
ILAFI	ILAF Intelligence
ILDF	Israel Defense Force
ILDF Front A	HQ north sector facing Lebanon, Syria and Iraq
ILDF Front B	HQ Samaria sector facing Iraq and Jordan
ILDF Front C	HQ Judea sector facing Jordan and Egypt
ILDF Front D	HQ south sector facing Egypt and Jordan
ILDF G Branch	General Staff Branch
ILFM	Israel Foreign Minister
ILNF	Israel Naval Force (Navy)
ILPM	Israel Prime Minister
OPOR	Operation Order
ORBAT	Order of Battle
PC	Personal Collection
PXNE	*Phoenix over the Nile, a history of Egyptian air power 1932-1994*, Lon Nordeen and David Nicolle, 1996
RAF	Royal Air Force
RTB	Return to Base
TOT	Time On Target
UK	United Kingdom
UN	United Nations
USA	United States of America
USSR	Union of Soviet Socialist Republics

Brief Background

UN Resolution 181, adopted on 29 November 1947, called for the partition of Palestine between an Arab State and a Jewish State with the British Mandate to end on 14 May 1948. Armed struggle between Arabs and Jews erupted immediately after the adoption of UN Resolution 181 as British forces prepared for withdrawal from Palestine and Arab League nations prepared to invade Palestine.

Israel's Independence was announced on 14 May 1948 and an Arab League invasion started the following day. The first round of the war lasted until a UN truce was imposed in June 1948. Arab expeditionary forces gained ground but failed to accomplish the Arab League objective of a swift invasion of Israel.

The second round of the war was an Israeli summer offensive during July 1948. The ILDF summer offensive was not wholly successful but it signaled that Arab expeditionary forces lost initial momentum while Israel assumed the offensive initiative.

The third round of the war was an Israeli autumn offensive during October 1948. The ILDF autumn offensive was partially successful and secured Israel territorial integrity with Galilee in the north and Negev in the south.

The fourth round of the war was an Israeli winter offensive that lasted from 22 December 1948 until 7 January 1949 and was known to ILDF as Operation HOREV.

OPOR HOREV

ILDF Front D HQ issued OPOR HOREV on 20 December 1948. Main participating forces were Brigade 1, Brigade 3, Brigade 8, Brigade 12 and elements of Brigade 10. HOREV's objective was the defeat of EGDF in Israel.

The main effort was an advance of Brigade 8 and Brigade 12, plus elements of Brigade 10, in the direction of Auja and Abu Ageila.

The secondary effort was a Brigade 1 attack against EGDF in Gaza, Rafah and the El Arish sector.

Brigade 10 was in reserve while Brigade 3 was tasked to preserve a blockade of the Faluja Pocket.

HOREV timetable was:
22 December 1948 dusk	ILAF attack
22 – 23 December 1948	Brigade 1 attack

24 – 25 December 1948   Brigade 12 attack
25 December 1948 dawn   Brigade 8 attack Auja

ILAF was tasked to accomplish air superiority and provide air support. Preplanned operations were:

Day	Time	Force	Attack
0	1645	3 B-17s	El Arish
0	1650	2 C-47s	Rafah
0	1650	1 C-46	Rafah
0	1650	2 T-6s	Gaza
0	1650	2 T-6s	Khan Yunes
0	1650	4 Pipers	Faluja
0	2100	1 C-46	Gaza
0	2230	1 C-47	El Arish
0	2300	1 C-47	El Arish
1	0100	1 C-46	Gaza
1	0400	1 C-47	El Arish
1	0415	1 C-47	Gaza
1	0500	1 C-46	Gaza
1	0930	3 B-17s	El Arish
1	1650	4 T-6s	Khan Yunes

Squadron 101 was tasked to patrol and photograph. Squadron 2 and Squadron 3 – the former moved from Dorot to Beer Sheba on 21 December 1948; the latter deployed from Ramat David to Tel Nof on 20 December 1948 – were to fly observation and liaison.

Military Balance

ILDF evaluation of the Egyptian expeditionary force in the HOREV sector was three regular brigades and nine reserve battalions; a force that was estimated at 10,000 to 13,000 soldiers. An EGDF brigade under siege at Faluja and Egyptian forces in Judea were not included in the ILDF evaluation of EGDF in the HOREV sector.

ILDF fielded 12 brigades divided between four fronts. Front D HOREV forces included five brigades, of which one faced the Faluja Pocket, one was assigned to a secondary effort against the Gaza Strip and three were assigned to the main effort in the direction of Auja.

ILAF evaluation of EGAF ORBAT was two Spitfire squadrons, two FIAT squadrons, one Stirling squadron and two transport squadrons.

ILAF ORBAT included some 60 aircraft assigned to seven squadrons and one flight at five bases:

Base	Unit	Type	Aircraft	Total
Ramat David	Squadron 69	B-17	1601	
			1602	
			1603	3
	Squadron 103	C-47	1401	
			1403	
			1405	3
		Beaufighter	Dalet172	1
			2202	
Dov Field	Squadron 1	Piper	0402	
			0412	2
		Bonanza	0602	
			0603	2
		Norecrin	0701	
			0702	2
		Rapide	1301	
			1302	
			1304	
			1305	
			1306	5
Tel Nof	Flight 35	C-64	Bet55/0804	1
		T-6	1101	
			1102	
			1103	
			1104	
			1105	
			1106	
			1107	7
	Squadron 3	Auster	0103	
			0106	
			0108	
			0110	
			0114	5
		Piper	0405	
			0406	
			0407	
			0409	4
		Fairchild	0501	1
	Squadron 106	C-46	RX-130/1701	
Base	Unit	Type	Aircraft	Total
			RX-131/1702	
			RX-133/1704	
			RX-137/1707	
			RX-138/1708	
			RX-136/1709	6
Hatzor	Squadron 101	Piper	0419	1
		Seabee	0901	
			1902	
			S199	
			1903	
			1904	
			1905	
			1906	7
		Spitfire	2001/10	
			2002/11	
			2003/12	
			2004/14	4

The ILAF changed its aircraft serial system in November 1948; the new serial system composed of four digits: the two left digits indicated type and the two right digits identified aircraft. Type 01 was Auster so 0115 was the 15th Auster in ILAF service at the time of new serial system introduction. Auster 0115 - reportedly photographed at St Jean, ILAF Flying School base, during December 1948 - was one of some 40 aircraft that were not assigned to frontline units at the start of HOREV; most of these aircraft were undergoing maintenance while others were awaiting disposal or assigned to the Flying School.

		P-51	2301/40	
			2302/41	2
Beer Sheba	Squadron 2	Piper	0401	
			0403	
			0404	
			0408	4

DAY 0
22 DECEMBER 1948

ILPM David Ben-Gurion originally preferred, in the wake of the ILDF autumn offensive, a Front B winter offensive against Iraqi forces in the Samaria sector, then suggested a Front C offensive against Jordanian forces in the Judea sector and finally settled for a Front D offensive against Egyptian forces in the Negev. On the morning of 22 December 1948, the ILPM was in Jerusalem, toured fortifications around the city together with Front C Commander Moshe Dayan and wrote in his diary:

> [Mount] Miss Carey [Ora] is one of the most wonderful beauty spots in Israel with a view of the Mediterranean Sea [to the west] and Moab Mountains [to the east] and with all [enemy] strongpoints south of Jerusalem spread out in front of us... it is tempting to occupy these [strongppoints]; after all, the natural border of Israel is [River] Jordan; we will have to see what will happen in the Negev during the coming days.

AMBUSH OVER EL ARISH

0520–0705	1	0402	Meiri	observation Front D
0650–0718	3	0409	Hirsh	Tel Nof Dov Field
0815–1005	101	0419	Axelrod	Hatzor Tel Nof Dov Field Hatzor
089–0940	3	0103	Moller	Tel Nof Dov Field Tel Nof
0915–0950	3	0405	Simantov	training
0931–0945	35	1103	Soltau	Hatzor Tel Nof
0935–1015	101	0901	Goodlin	Hatzor Tel Nof Dov Field Hatzor
0955–1039	3	0501	Biram	training
0958–1016	35	1103	Brown	Tel Nof Dov Field
1010–1100	1	0402) 0412)		Efrat Kahana training
1015–1335	1	1305	Kaplan	Dov Field St Jean Ramat David Dov Field
1020–1135	101	0419	Axelrod	Hatzor Tel Nof Hatzor
1047–1103	3	0501	Biram	training
1100–1145	1	0603	Machnes Lahat	training
1105–1223	3	0407		training
1115–1205	1	0402) 0412)		Efrat Porat training
1150–1250	101	2001/10	Augarten	reconnaissance, scramble
1210–1240	101	2004/14	Doyle	scramble

Squadron 101 was tasked to fly a reconnaissance mission but enemy aircraft were sighted and the Spitfires were scrambled to intercept:

The ILAF official kill credit certifies that Squadron 101 pilot Rudy Augarten, in Spitfire D-130 (which was marked 2001/10 at the time), shot down an Egyptian FIAT over El Arish on 22 December 1948.

As pilot was taking off for a photo recce he was scrambled after the enemy aircraft that were sighted south of base. Pilot proceeded to reported airfield south of El Arish... pilot proceeded to El Arish airfield. As pilot approached El Arish... observed one aircraft, landing, to the southeast of the long runway. Then he observed a FIAT G55 starting to turn in on its base leg with his wheels down. Pilot dived down and fired several bursts at him. Then pilot over rode him and made another pass as the FIAT turned into his approach leg. Observed strikes on the FIAT at this time. Pilot overrode him again and when he last saw him he observed that the FIAT had rolled off of the end of the long runway and was still rolling (turning towards the right) when he was last seen. Pilot then returned to base.

ILAF identified all EGAF Italian fighters as FIAT but, reportedly, the involved aircraft was a Macchi 205 and the injured pilot was Shalabi Hinnawy. Though the EGAF aircraft was seen to land, damaged but in one piece, ILAF credited Augarten with a kill.

OWL ACTIVATION

1155–1235	1	1302	Steinman	test bombing
1210–1340	1	0603	Machnes Lahat	Dov Field Ramat David Dov Field
1325–1515	35	1103	Soltau	Hatzor Tel Nof Dov Field Tel Nof
1420–1630	1	0402	Levitin	Dov Field Ramat David Dov Field

In order to improve ILDF, ILAF and ILNF cooperation during HOREV, OWL HQ – situated inside ILAF HQ – was activated at 1300.

RAID EL ARISH

1450–1650	69	1603	Raisin Noach Harris Cuburnek Goldstein Lichtman Aronson Meyerson Duboff Gershaw Joffe	attack El Arish with 30*100lb+2* 250kg bombs
1458–1658	69	1602	Feldman Ratushniak Jacobs Michel Soltan Fink Lowenberg Lazarus Nash Jackson	attack El Arish with 30*100lb bombs
1500–1515	1	0412	Steinman	test
1500–1620	2	0403	Ospovat	observation Auja
1520–1640	101	2003/12	Weizman	escort Squadron 69
1520–1640	101	2004/14	Wilson	ditto

Squadron 69 Commander Al Raisin flew in the lead at the opening of the Operation HOREV air raid in B-17 1603 that was, at the time, still referred to as '693'; the bomber was photographed, in mixed markings, wearing both old 693 and new 1603, over Ramat David.

693 attacked EGAF air base from 1604 until 1606, from 15,000 feet. Bombardier Jules Cuburnek reported that 250 kilograms bombs hit south of the runways intersection and a string of smaller bombs hit across the runways. A gunner reported observation of a seemingly destroyed C-47 near the runway intersection, perhaps the C-47 that belly-landed at El Arish on 4 November 1948.

1602 followed from 1606 until 1607, at 16,000 feet with hits observed east of the runways intersection. A light brown colored C-47 was reported west of the runways intersection, probably the same seemingly destroyed C-47.

Squadron 101 pilots also noted the C-47 and reported:

> Observed the bombs fall across the two runways near the intersection; approximately two bursts on each of the runways.

Both B-17 crews reported fine weather and good visibility with no clouds over the target; AAA fire was inaccurate. 1602's debrief concluded with the following plea:

> Crew complains insufficient warm clothing. Adequate gloves, socks and boots must be obtained. Crew's fingers sorely affected. Silk and chamois gloves needed.

RAID KHANYUNES

1519–1625	35	1106	Gibson	attack Khan Yunes with 8★50kg bombs
1519–1622	35	1105	Flint	ditto
1520–1629	35	1102	Soltau	attack Khan Yunes with 8★30kg bombs
1520–1627	35	1101	Dougherty	ditto
1535–1635	101	1903	Cohen	escort Flight 35
1535–1630	101	1904	Goodlin	ditto

Attacked from 1604, escorts reported:

> Did not see AT-6s after take-off and proceeded straight to target. There observed three AT-6s over the target, bombing, and provided escort. Plane 2 tested his guns and shot holes in two blades of his propeller and RTB. Plane 1 observed the Harvards bombing... and saw the bombs fall in the sand outside of tented camp, in the camp and in edge of town. Pilot

The standard offensive load for Flight 35 T-6 was eight 50kg bombs.

then escorted two of the Harvards back to base, the third one not seen after the bombing.

RAID FALUJA RAFAH

1545–1611	3	0106	Biram	Tel Nof Ramat David
1558–1758	103	1401	Rosin Agmon	attack Rafah with Kenny Manor 16★100kg bombs
1630–1709	3	0407	Dankner	attack Faluja with 3★18kg bombs
1635–1655	3	0406	Goldstein	attack Faluja with 8★18kg bombs

Goldstein attacked from 3,000 feet and Dankner followed. 1401 was over Rafah from 1705 until 1709; faced heavy and medium AAA; reported very good visibility and good weather without clouds over target. Agmon wrote:

> Reached target at last light, 10,000 feet, dived and bombed at 8,000 [feet]...

A debrief remark was:

> Demand fighter escort on day raids.

END OF DAY 0

1640–1705	1	0412	Kaplan Kraft	training
1645–1850	1	0603	Lahat Machnes	Dov Field Ramat David Dov Field
1905–2040	1	0603	Machnes Lahat	Dov Field Ramat David Dov Field
2255–2400	1	1305	Machnes Efrat	training

OPOR HOREV tasked ILAF to dispatch 17 attack sorties during Day 0 with TOT from 1645 until 2300. So far, nine ILAF Day 0 attack sorties have been unearthed:

Two B-17s raided El Arish air base from 1604 – HOREV plan was for three B-17s with TOT at 1645.

Four T-6s dive-bombed KhanYunes from 1604 – HOREV plan was for two T-6s to attack Gaza and two T-6s to attack Khan Yunes with TOT at 1650.

Two Pipers harassed Faluja circa sunset at 1645 – HOREV plan was

The ILDF plan for HOREV included a raid against El Arish air base, with ILAF dropping paratroopers prior to the raid and ILNF evacuating paratroopers after the raid, but this plan was not executed so Squadron 106 C-46s flew transport and bombing missions during HOREV but did not drop paratroopers.

for four Pipers with TOT at 1650.

One C-47 bombed Rafah from 1705 – HOREV plan was for one C-46 and two C-47s with TOT at 1650.

Additional HOREV Day 0 planned sorties were one C-46 to bomb Gaza at 2100, one C-47 to raid El Arish at 2230 and one C-47 to bomb El Arish at 2300. The C-47s were delayed while a logbook entry indicated that Isaac Henenson and Michael Keren bombed Gaza in RX-137 on the evening of 22 December 1948, but such a sortie is not mentioned in Tel Nof log of flights nor in any known reference.

The impact of ILAF attacks is difficult to define. Reports that HOREV Day 0 bombing of El Arish air base resulted in the destruction of a C-47 and a FIAT are probably inaccurate since the 'FIAT' was engaged in a pre-HOREV H Hour mission and the C-47 was not destroyed during HOREV Day 0 bombing of El Arish but reported as a wreckage.

DAY 1
23 DECEMBER 1948

Brigade 1 Battalion 13 initiated HOREV ground action with an attack in direction of Hill 86 – roughly midway between Gaza and Rafah – aimed at cutting off Egyptian forces in the Gaza Strip as well as to create a diversion from HOREV's main effort at Auja sector. ILAF was tasked to dispatch four bombing sorties from midnight to sunset of Day 1 but a few Day 0 bombing sorties were delayed and actually flown during Day 1.

RAID EL ARISH RAFAH

2340–0412   103   1401   Katz Berliand Festing Kemp attack El Arish with 16*100kg bombs

There were reports of very bad weather from Ramat David to Tel Aviv and good weather from Tel Aviv to El Arish, with very good visibility over the target. The actual target was El Arish air base but this was not pinpointed, so 1401 diverted to Rafah as an alternative target, was over target from 0126 until 0145, bombed from 10,000 feet and reported:

> Captain: original target was not identified; hastily bombed what was believed to be Rafah. Over El Arish an explosion was heard and an orange flame was seen below aircraft. Discovery of enemy fighter prevented us from making a more thorough search for target. Enemy aircraft sighted by two crew members. The aircraft was believed to be twin-engined. No flak or searchlight over what believed to be El Arish or Rafah. Searchlight playing on the water near Gaza; no ships sighted. Radio Operator: Saw an aircraft; informed the pilot. Joined by navigator and pointed the aircraft out to him. He confirmed. Took violent evasive action but the aircraft managed to tail us for quite a long distance. We lost sight of him outside Gaza when the pilot did a 360 [degrees] turn over the sea [at] (1,000 feet).
> Navigator: Identified the plane as twin-engined.
> Pilot: Confirms the above.

As a result of the search for El Arish and due to the reported encounter with enemy aircraft, the C-47 landed at Tel Nof at 0201, refueled and returned to Ramat David at 0412.

RAID EL ARISH RAFAH

2357–0434   103   1405   Shatkai Nathan attack El Arish with Weinstein Aronson 16*100kg bombs

Also tasked to raid El Arish, also unable to pinpoint target and also diverted to attack Rafah from 0153 until 0154; is it possible that 1405 was the enemy aircraft that 1401 reported? 1405 pilot reported:

> Arrived west of target. Could not locate target properly because of lack of petrol. No signs of activity at El Arish, no searchlights or AAA. Went to Rafah; to the south of Rafah there were eight searchlights; located some dim lights and bombed them. Proceeded to Tel Nof, landing with 40 gallons of petrol.

The C-47 landed at Tel Nof at 0224, refueled and proceed to Ramat David where it landed at 0434. Crew concluded debrief with four complaints:

> - Quantity of petrol about 400 gallons, which does not allow for a climb of 10,000 feet or any emergency.
> - Met briefing extremely inaccurate – cloud of 8,000 feet thickness, rain, hail and icing.
> - Hang up; one of the bombs did not drop despite double effort at jettisoning.
> - Nothing to marshal the aircraft at Ramat David in a blinding rain.

RAID GAZA FALUJA

0230–0339   106   RX-133   attack Gaza with 20*50kg bombs
0241–0339   3   0405   (Goldstein) attack Faluja with 8*18kg bombs
0243–0454   3   0407   (Dankner) attack Faluja with 8*20kg bombs

EGAF apparently retaliated circa 0400 when Tel Nof was bombed; ILAF reported three bombs with no casualties or damage while Adam Shatkai, pilot of 1405, reported:

Took off from Tel Nof and on take-off the field was raided. Numerous hits could be seen in the vicinity (seven hits observed for sure).

VELVETTA SPITFIRES

0730–0830	2	Piper	Portugali	observation Auja Rafah
0800–0950	2	Piper	Ospovat	observation Auja
0927–0947	3	0110	Giladi	Tel Nof Dov Field
0954–1520	106	RX-130	Lewis Foster Cohen Shimoni Bloch	VELVETTA 2 Niksic Tel Nof lead ship
			Styrack Goodelman McElroy	
1000–1510	101	2009	Lichter	VELVETTA 2 Niksic Tel Nof
1000–1514	101	2011	Shapira	VELVETTA 2 Niksic Tel Nof
1000–1515	101	2008	Dangott	VELVETTA 2 Niksic Hatzor
1000–1518	101	2012	Hod	VELVETTA 2 Niksic Tel Nof
1000–1100	101	2013	Ruch	VELVETTA 2 Niksic Niksic, abort, RTB
1030–1230	2	Piper	Rubens	observation Bir Asluj
1039–1050	35	Bet55/0804		Sunderland test
1155–1435	1	0603	Lahat	Dov Field Ramat David Dov Field
1220–1528	106	RX-136	Krokstedt	VELVETTA 2 search and rescue aircraft
1230–1355	101	2002/11	Senior	patrol Khan Yunes Rafah El Arish
1235–1400	101	2004/14	Levett	ditto
1240–1300	1	1302	Kaplan	test
1430–1450	3	0409	Front	Dov Field Tel Nof
1430–1615	1	0402	Efrat	Dov Field Ramat David Dov Field
1455–1520	101	2302/41	Doyle	VELVETTA 2 escort
1500–1520	101	2001	Feldman	ditto

Squadron 101 initiated HOREV with only five S199s, four Spitfires and two P-51s. ILAF planned to reinforce Squadron 101, in time for HOREV, with 12 Spitfires that were to be flown to Israel from Czechoslovakia, via Yugoslavia. Operation VELVETTA 2 was planned to include two flights, from Czechoslovakia to Israel, of six Spitfires each, but these were delayed due to bad weather. Six Spitfires were at Niksic, Yugoslavia, by morning of 23 December 1948 but one was unserviceable, so McElroy boarded the C-46 lead ship. Five Spitfires departed Niksic but Ruch's 2013 malfunctioned after some 30 minutes so he turned back and returned to Niksic. Four Spitfires arrived at Israel. Three landed, as planned, at Tel Nof for AMU acceptance inspection; the other landed, not as planned, at Hatzor.

RAIN AND RETREAT

1617–1645	3	0405	Goldstein	training
1618–1648	3	0409	Simantov	training
1638–1703	35	1101	Dougherty	attack Faluja with 8*50kg bombs
1639–1704	35	1102	Soltau	ditto
1639–1705	35	1105	Flint	ditto
1642–1706	35	1106	Gibson	ditto
1901–1918	106	RX-133	Lewis	test

Two VELVETTA 2 Spitfires - believed to be 2009 and 2011 - flying from Yugoslavia to Israel on 23 December 1948.

Squadron 106 C-46 pilot Ray Foster poses beside the VELVETTA 2 Spitfire 2011 prior to flight from Yugoslavia to Israel.

Squadron 101 pilot Caesar Dangott on the VELVETTA 2 Spitfire - with two underwing fuel tanks and one belly tank - at Niksic, Yugoslavia, prior to flight to Israel.

Rain started over Tel Aviv during the night of 22 to 23 December 1948, and although it would only start raining in the south from the evening of 23 December, ILAF operations slowed down; the only ILAF Day 1 daylight offensive operation was Flight 35 attacking Faluja.

Front D reported retreat from Hill 86 at 1815; an Egyptian counterattack pushed back Battalion 13 and frustrated the ILDF plan to wedge a strip of land between Gaza and Rafah. The same Front D message also reported pouring rain at Beer Sheba.

DAY 2
24 DECEMBER 1948

Brigade 8, Brigade 10 and Brigade 12 were at the holding area, ready to start the HOREV main effort, but poor weather delayed their attack; in anticipation of the HOREV main effort, the ILAF stepped-up offensive operations.

MIDNIGHT TO DAWN

0215–0326	103	1405	Boshes Keidar Millman Laron Boettger Greenberger Stern attack Gaza with 16*100kg bombs
0350–1120	106	RX-137	Applebaum VELVETTA 2 Tel Nof Niksic

1405 reported poor weather; it arrived over the target at 10,500 feet still inside clouds, could not pinpoint target and so jettisoned bombs over the Mediterranean Sea, some 15 miles west of Tel Aviv, then RTB.

DAWN TO MIDDAY

0612–0716	35	1106	Gibson	attack Dir Balah
0612–0715	35	1102	Soltau	ditto
0613–0717	35	1105	Flint	ditto
0635–0900	1	0402	Steinman	Dov Field Ramat David Dov Field
0710–0800	101	2302/41	Augarten	patrol Khan Yunes Rafah El Arish
0740–0755	3	0103	Moller	Tel Nof Dov Field
0930–1122	69	1602	Katz Ben Porat Bresslof Weissbrod attack Khan Yunes with 15*100kg+ 20*50kg bombs Ber Cohen Jacobson Swiel Spicehandler Kahn	
0931–1122	69	1603)	McConville Maseng Weinstein Seftel attack Khan Yunes with 16*100lb+ 16*FRAG bombs Robinson Liponetzky Wadman Cohen Schwartzbach Joffe	

Rudy Augarten flew P-51 Dalet191 on the morning of 24 December 1948; it was still reported as Dalet191 even though reidentified as 2302 during November 1948.

Following the introduction of the new ILAF serial system during November 1948, Squadron 101 introduced an in-house unofficial tactical code system that resembled US 12th Air Force's Second World War system; in the US 12th Air Force system the numbers 10 to 39 were the codes of the first squadron in a wing and the numbers 40 to 69 were the codes of the second squadron in a wing; in the Squadron 101 system the numbers 10 to 39 were reserved for Spitfires and the numbers from 40 onwards to P-51s so that 2302, ex Dalet191, was also 41.

DAY 2: 24 DECEMBER 1948

0940–1015	1	0603	Machnes Eyal	training
1005–1120	101	2001/10	Feldman	escort Squadron 69
1005–1120	101	2002/11	Doyle	ditto
1010–1110	101	2302/41	Goodlin	patrol Mediterranean Sea north of El Arish
1030–1325	1	0402	Levitin	Dov Field St Jean Ramat David Dov Field
1050–1105	101	0419		training
1120–1220	1	0603	Machnes Eyal	Dov Field Hatzor Dov Field
1155–1235	1	1302	Steinman	test bombing
1200–1405	1	1305	Renov	Dov Field St Jean Dov Field

Augarten first flew over El Arish, where he observed that the long runway seemed serviceable and that along the short runway there were, possibly, one or two craters, while three fighters were also spotted. Augarten then pinpointed a previously-unknown EGAF air base at El Riah, south of El Arish and nearby Bir Lahfan, where three fighters in pens were observed.

Squadron 69 was tasked to bomb Khan Yunes. The weather was described as fair and the two bombers initiated an attack, from 13,000 feet, at 1038. Katz's first run was a dummy due to clouds; during the second run, three bombs were observed to explode in the center of town but there were 30 hang-ups so Katz flew to Gaza, where the bombardier could not drop the bombs so the armorer released two bombs by hand and the remaining bombs were jettisoned over the sea. McConville reported that bombing was inaccurate due to clouds over the target.

MIDDAY TO DUSK

1335–1355	1	1302	Steinman	test bombing
1340–1150	1	0603	Machnes Avisar	training
1412–1612	103		Beaufighter	Berliand Gochen attack El Riah with 6*100lb bombs
1430–1730	1	0402	Lahat Simon	observation Auja
1445–1545	101	1906	Augarten	escort Squadron 103
1445–1550	101	Dalet123	Senior	ditto
1500–1600	2	Piper	Portugali	observation Bir Asluj
1522–1652	69	B-17	Feldman Ratushniak Jacobs Michel attack Gaza with 28*D70 bombs Fink Lowenberg Soltan Lazarus Jackson Nash Joffe	
1545–1655	69	1601	Raisin Noach Harris Cuburnek attack Gaza with 14*D70 bombs Goldstein Aronson Duboff Meyerson Gershaw Lichtman	
1600–1650	101	0419		Hatzor Tel Nof Hatzor
1610–1735	1	0603	Renov	Dov Field Hatzor Tel Nof Dov Field
1615–1715	2	0412		observation Bir Asluj Auja Rafah
1620–1715	35	1102		attack Khan Yunes with 8*50kg bombs
1620–1715	35	1104		ditto
1620–1715	35	1105		ditto
1655–1715	1	0602	Machnes	test

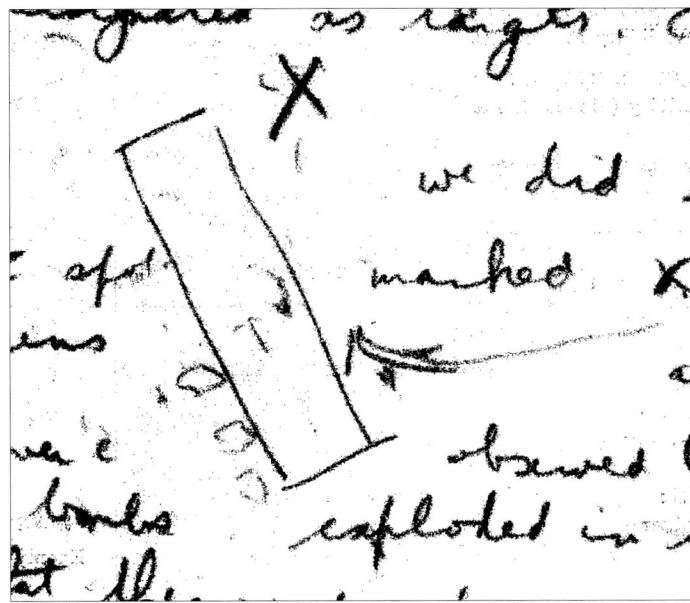

A sketch of El Riah from 24 December 1948 - Squadron 101's mission debrief.

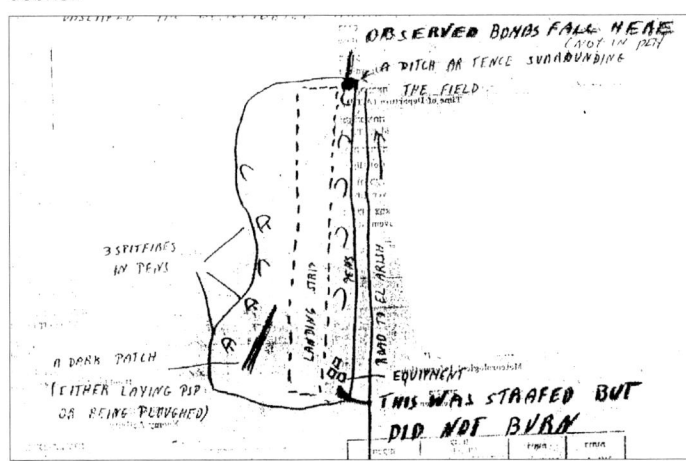

A sketch of El Riah from 24 December 1948 - Squadron 103's mission debrief (less informative but generally similar.

ILAF HQ Operations officer Smoky Simon, who flew as an observer with Squadron 1 Commander Shlomo Lahat, wrote:

> Set course from Nebi Rubin via Dorot, Imara to Auja. Hit rain just north Auja. Recced at 5,000 feet (4,000 feet above ground). Circa 120 vehicles parked in five dispersals. Dug in positions and trenches in area and Auja itself. Four trucks moving on road to Ismailia (Egypt) and three on road to Bir Asluj. Recced road from Auja to Bir Asluj. Counted circa 75 vehicles parked in dispersals, circa six moving near Bir Asluj. Saw Burma road built by Egyptians at Bir Asluj. North of Bir Asluj is large camp with circa 20 vehicles, this is the most northerly Egyptian positions between Bir Asluj and Beer Sheba. Flew to Beer Sheba. Our [Squadron 2 air]field unserviceable due to rain. Contact with Squadron 2 on walkie-talkie. RTB via Faluja.

Squadron 103 Beaufighter was tasked to raid EGAF at El Riah that Augarten had pinpointed earlier that day; Augarten flew lead with the Beaufighter following the S199s to El Riah. The Squadron 101 escort pilots reported poor visibility over the target while the Beaufighter crew reported good weather and good visibility over the target; this shows that weather can be subjective. S199 pilots reported TOT from 1510 until 1525, while Beaufighter crew reported it as from 1525

The line of five S199s at Hatzor with Dalet123, which flew the mission to Auja on 24 December 1948, nearest the camera.

until 1526. The S199 pilots spotted three 'Spitfires' in pens, observed the Beaufighter's bombs exploding north-east of the runway and reported that the Beaufighter strafed equipment south-east of the runway. Both S199 pilots and the Beaufighter crew reported absence of AAA fire and no EGAF activity.

Squadron 69 B-17s bombed Gaza from 1604 until 1605 and from 1621 until 1623. Feldman's crew reported fair weather and bad visibility over the target that was attacked from 15,500 feet in the face of inaccurate AAA fire. Raisin's crew reported good weather with good visibility over the target and bombed from 13,000 feet in the face of accurate AAA fire that appeared to follow the B-17 but did not hit it.

Flight 35 raided Khan Yunes from 1650 until 1710. ILAFI reported:

> Visibility over target was bad. Aircraft became separated and because of bad weather, accurate bombing was difficult. Leading aircraft returned to Faluja and made hits on west side of town. Definite hits on town were observed. Second aircraft bombed Dir Balah area but due to bad visibility could not observe result of bombing. The bombload of the third plane were dropped in twos in the Khan Yunes, Dir Balah area. The crew did not observe hits. Heavy ack ack was encountered over Gaza, medium over Dir Balah, medium over Khan Yunes and light (20 mm) over Faluja.

Also flying reconnaissance in preparation for the launch of the HOREV main effort was 0412, which was specifically tasked to evaluate the condition of canyons. ILAFI reported:

> Visibility was good. Some water was flowing in Wadi Asluj. In the Wadi Abyad near Auja no water was seen. Seven trucks were observed traveling from Rafah to Auja.

END OF DAY 2

| 1945–2205 | 1 | 1305 | Kaplan | Dov Field Ramat David Dov Field |
| 2050–2105 | 103 | Samekh82 | Katz | Ramat David Tel Nof |

The ILPM visited Front D HQ, suggested to explore HOREV opportunity to eliminate the Faluja Pocket and then, on the way from Gedera to Beer Sheba, experienced the impact of floods in Negev; the ILPM convoy successfully crossed two canyons but their Jeeps drowned in the third canyon they attempted to cross, so the ILPM walked to a nearby road, stopped a Jeep and was hitched to Beer Sheba!

At Beer Sheba, the ILPM learnt that due to rains, the start of HOREV main effort was delayed from the night of 24 to 25 December 1948 to the night of 25 to 26 December.

From HOREV Day 0 to Day 2, ILAF operations were not met with any aerial resistance; the only known EGAF reaction to HOREV during this timeframe were sporadic nocturnal bombings that continued during the evening of 24 December. Ramat David was bombed at 2115, as ILAFI reported:

> About eight bombs were dropped, some of them apparently 500 pounders. There were no casualties and damage was light.

Beit Jibrin, an ILDF outpost north-east of Beer Sheba, was bombed at 2200, as ILAFI reported:

> There were no casualties, nor was there any damage.

Also circa 2200, an unidentified aircraft bombed Jericho and the nearby palace of King Abdullah. Jordan blamed enemy aircraft but did not say to which enemy the bomber belonged. Israel stated that the ILAF did not operate over Jordan during the night of 24 to 25 December, speculated that the bomber was Egyptian and that the bombing was the result of an innocent navigation error or the outcome of a pre-planned provocation, aimed to force Jordan to resume fighting against Israel at a time when Israel attacked Egypt and Jordan initiated a clandestine negotiation with Israel. A realistic evaluation of this bombing was reported by the USA Embassy in Amman:

> Amman... gave the King's comment that the air raid on Jericho and [King Palace at] Shuneh... may have been carried out by Egyptians. Bomb fragment bore words [Egypt King] Farouk to [ILFM] Shertock in the Arabic letters. [FRUS]

An unrealistic but interesting Jordanian point of view was

subsequently communicated to Washington from the USA Embassy in Amman:

> Certain evidence now points to air raid on Jericho being carried by Jewish plane with bombs captured from Egyptians. Raid may have been for psychological purposes as bombs were dropped in such a manner as to cause no damage. British RAF in Egypt have reported they satisfied it not Egyptian plane. [FRUS]

Mishmar Ha Emek, a kibbutz some five kilometers south of Ramat David, was bombed at 2230; one woman and three children were killed, and five were injured. The bomber or bombers, reportedly EGAF Stirling or Stirlings, was or were still heard over Haifa at 2315 but the ILAF lacked night fighters and was unable to intercept the EGAF bombers.

DAY 3
25 DECEMBER 1948

HOREV's secondary effort had already failed and the main effort was delayed due to winter weather. ILAF activity focused on attack, observation, patrol, reconnaissance and transport. Support missions were not flown, not even when Battalion 13 came under Egyptian daylight counter-attack on 23 December and was forced to retreat from Hill 86 with heavy losses.

In line with the ILPM's suggestion to eliminate the Faluja Pocket during HOREV, an ILDF artillery bombardment and ILAF air raids were initiated during Day 3; the objective was to soften the Faluja Pocket in advance of an attack, though this change of plan resulted in two parallel main efforts – the ILDF always preferred one main effort at a time.

RAID FALUJA

0424–0605	103	1405	Rosin Agmon Segal Lipman
			attack Faluja with 16*100kg bombs
			Erlich Berger Hollander
0550–0525	3	0405	attack Faluja with 12*3kg bombs
0720–0816	3	0405	Simantov training
0910–0925	1	1304	Machnes test

Pouring rain in the Negev Desert slowed down HOREV operations.

Squadron 103 and Squadron 3 initiated the bombing of Faluja almost simultaneously. 0405 bombed Faluja airfield from 0510 until 0515 and reported hazy visibility, all bombs on target, fires in Faluja town and machine-gun fire. 1405 followed from 0513 to 0524, reporting poor visibility and poor weather, with cloud base at 5,500 feet, and bombed from 3,800 feet:

> Two runs after identifying target. First run [heading] 120 degrees. All incendiaries thrown and a stick of 10 [bombs] released from racks. Stick fell parallel to road Faluja Manshiya, in northern sector of town. Bombs were seen and felt on explosion... Second run, same heading. Six bombs fell on west center of town... all bombs exploded. When leaving target, small fires seen burning.

The 1405 crew added the following observations:

> - Searchlight at Gaza active.
> - Tel Aviv excellent waypoint due to being lit up.
> - Ships in [Tel Aviv] Port resembling Hanuka Menorah.
> - Kfar Joshua [west of Ramat David] did not learn from bombing and celebrated sabbath with lights on.

The debrief report ended with a wish:

> We would appreciate better liaison with army, for purposes of identifying target.

RECONNAISSANCE

0940–1045	101	2001/10	Augarten	photo Bir Burg
0940–1045	101	2002/11	Weizman	escort photo Bir Burg
1000–1200	2	0412	Cohen	observation
1002–1244	3	0405	Goldstein	Tel Nof Beer Sheba Dov Field Tel Nof
1010–1145	2	0408		observation Auja

Squadron 101 was tasked to photograph the area east and west of Bir Burg; pilots reported good visibility and ILAFI summed up:

> Having photographed target area, proceeded to reported [El Riah] airfield south of El Arish. Observed three Spitfires on field. Observed an ack ack position (possibly a battery)... Encountered inaccurate medium ack ack from Gaza and medium ack ack from El Arish.

RAID EL ARISH

1011–1230	69	1601	Raisin Shiftman Harris Cuburnek
			attack El Arish with 26*D70 bombs
			Aronson Goldstein Lichtman Meyerson
			Gershaw Duboff
1012–1232	69	1603	McConville Noach Seftel Weinstein
			attack El Arish with 25*D70 bombs
			Schwartzbach Cohen Kahn Robinson
			Cohen Liponetzky
1016–1108	3	0106	Giladi training
1020–1230	69	1602	Feldman Ratushniak Jacobs Michel

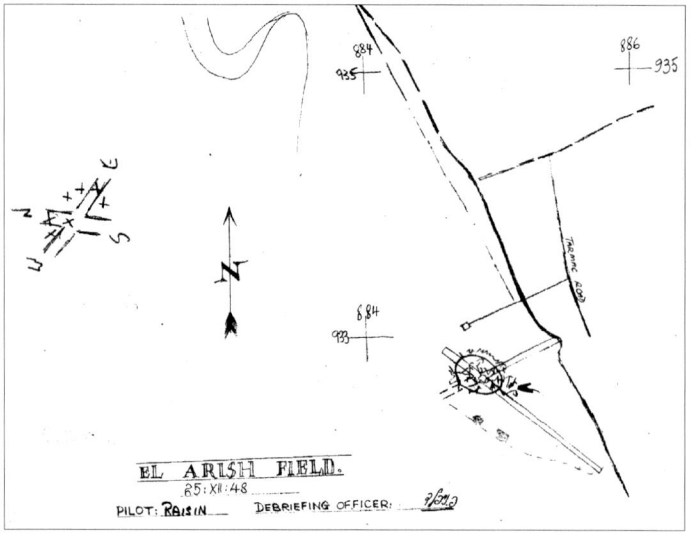

Squadron 69 Commander Al Raisin's debrief drawing of the 'perfect bombing' on El Arish air base on 25 December 1948.

				attack El Arish with 26*D70 bombs Soltan Lowenberg Fink Nash Jackson Lazarus
1030–1130	2	Piper	Halivni	observation (Auja)
1030–1230	2	0403	Portugali	observation Auja Abu Ageila
1035–1205	101	2003/12	Cohen	escort Squadron 69
1035–1245	101	2302/41	Senior	ditto
1045–1705	1	0402	Kahana	Dov Field Ramat David Tel Nof Dov Field
1055–1107	35	1103	Kaplansky	Tel Nof Dov Field
1055–1310	1	1304	Efrat	Dov Field Haifa Ramat David Dov Field
1135–1245	101	0419	Hatzor	Dov Field Hatzor
1200–1300	2	Piper	Zibel	training

Squadron 69 raided El Arish air base from 1125 until 1128. The B-17 crews reported good weather and bombed from 15,500 feet. AAA was "*fairly accurate*" and Feldman reported "*kite has one hole near right waist ¾in in diameter*". Raisin's crew debrief concluded with the statement:

> All bombs went. Bombs fell in an east-west direction bang across intersection of runways. Bomb hitting both runways and intersection of runways. Perfect bombing.

CAMEL CARAVAN

1216–1332	106	RX-136/1709	Ribacoff	test
1305–1515	1	1306	Steinman	Dov Field Ramat David Dov Field
1338–1425	3	0405	Dankner	training
1344–1351	3	0103	Giladi	Tel Nof (Beer Sheba) Tel Nof, abort, RTB
1350–1455	101	2001/10	Cohen	photo Auja
1350–1500	101	2002/11	Feldman	escort photo Auja
1418	3	0106	Giladi	Tel Nof Beer Sheba
1500–1700	2	0408	Cohen	observation
1500–1512	106	RX-133/1704	Ribacoff	test
1515–1625	3	0409	Dankner	Tel Nof Dov Field Tel Nof
1515–1550	101	2302/41	Weizman	patrol Mediterranean Sea
1515–1700	1	0602	Renov Avisar	Dov Field Ramat David Dov Field
1520–1630	101	0419	Hatzor	Dov Field Hatzor
1521–1605	3	0405	Brown	training
1530–1700	2	0403	Portugali	observation Faluja
1545–1555	1	0702	Solarsh	test
1600–1730	2	0404	Halivni	observation Bir Asluj

Squadron 101 pilots tasked with photographing Auja were over the target from 1415 to 1438; visibility was good and slight vehicle movement was observed. Squadron 101 pilot Ezer Weizman reported good visibility and no unusual activity during a patrol along the coastline, some 30 miles out to sea during the outbound leg and some 10 miles from the coastline during the return flight. Squadron 2 pilot Abraham Portugali was tasked to pinpoint a camel caravan going to Faluja. He reported poor visibility and the camel caravan was not found.

RAID RAFAH

1600–1800	69	1601	Raisin Shiftman Harris Cuburnek attack Rafah with 30*100lb bombs Aronson Lichtman Goldstein Meyerson Duboff Gershaw Joffe
1601–1755	69	1602	McConville Noach Seftel Weinstein attack Rafah with 30*100lb bombs Schwartzbach Cohen Liponetzky Cohen Robinson
1602–1743	69	1603	Katz BenPorat Bresslof Weissbrod attack Rafah with 27*100lb bombs Kahn Spicehandler Jackson Swiel Ber Tolkowsky

The B-17s flew a single bomb run at 14,500 feet, except for Katz who flew at 14,000 feet, from 1654 to 1655. Visibility was reported as fair and good; weather reports ranged from fair to good. Egyptian AAA was described as heavy, accurate, thick and plenty. Bombing by 1601 and 1603 was reportedly successful but 1602 broke off the attack and jettisoned its bombs over the Mediterranean, north-west of Tel Aviv, after the tail gunner saw "*two aircraft west of Gaza over sea*" while the waist gunner saw "*one aircraft at same place*". McConville reported:

> Fighters made pass so plane took evasive action out to sea.

None of the other airmen on-board 1601 and 1603 saw enemy aircraft, not one Israeli fighter was airborne at the time of the Squadron 69 raid, but the crew of 1603 reported hearing radio chatter in English:

> - Jack 1 calling Jack 2
> - Hearing you 1 by 1

Sunset was at 1646 and the crews devoted debriefings to criticize blackout over Israel. Raisin remarked:

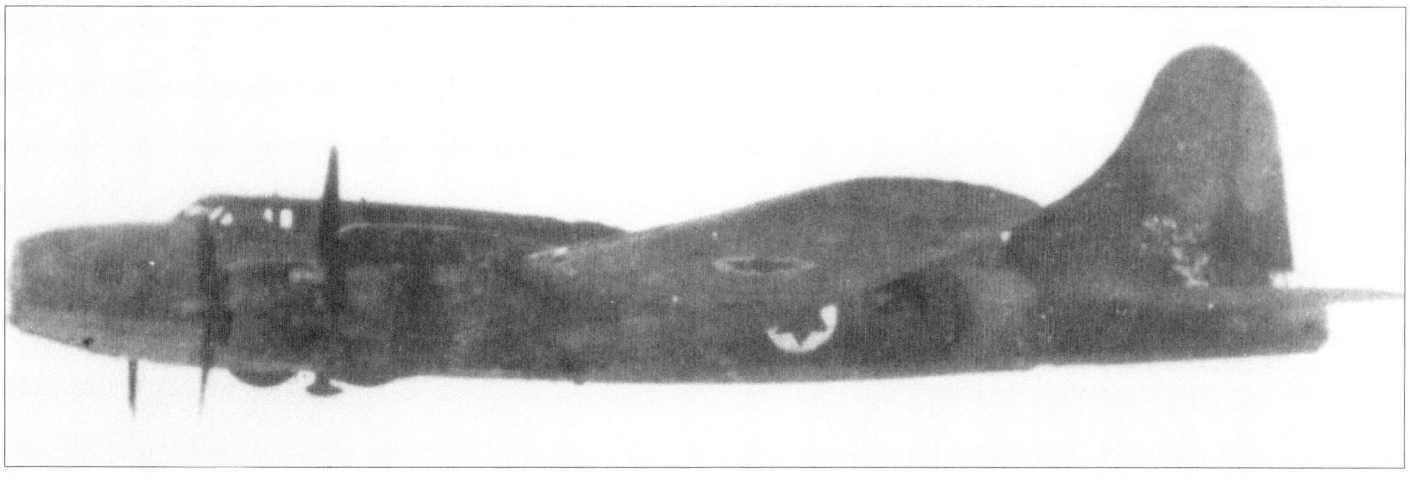
John McConville and crew in 1602 – photographed in flight – aborted an attack on Rafah during the afternoon of 25 December 1948 and jettisoned bombs after reporting enemy aircraft. Intercepted radio chatter in English may point out that these were British fighters on visual reconnaissance mission over the front.

Flight 35 pilot Eddie Kaplansky tested T-6 1103 from 1707 on 25 December 1948; though reidentified as ILAF 1103 since mid-November 1948, the previous identity Bet65 was still in use during December 1948.

Blackout (Israel) poor.

Harris added:

Kfar Joshua is presumed to be celebrating Xmas with Hanuka lights. This kibbutz [actually a village] is half a mile from west end of 270 runway.

Cuburnek concluded:

Tel Aviv and Haifa lit up like the Mardi Gras.

END OF DAY 3

1603–1617	3	0103	Ruff	test	
1650–1805	3	0405	Hirsh	Tel Nof Dov Field Tel Nof	
1700–1722	3	0409	Goldstein	observation Faluja	
1707–1715	35	1103	Kaplansky	test	
1800–1905	1	0702	Machnes	Dov Field Hatzor Dov Field	
1925–2115	1	0602	Machnes	Dov Field (Ramat David) Dov Field, RTB	
2400–0110	2	Piper	Halivni	(Beer Sheba) Dov Field	

Front D reported, at 1830, the start of forces' movements in the direction of Auja to initiate HOREV's main effort.

During Day 3, ILAF attacked Faluja, El Arish and Rafah, as well as flying observation, patrol, reconnaissance and transport missions. EGAF was still absent over the HOREV theater but again retaliated with nocturnal bombings. The area north-west of Ramat David was bombed at 2000 and, due to this bombing, Squadron 1 pilot Benjamin Machnes aborted a transport flight to Ramat David. Ras El Ain and Kfar Sirkin were attacked at 2250, as ILAFI reported:

Eleven 250-pound bombs are supposed to have been thrown in two sticks of four and seven. An unconfirmed report states that a C-46 did the bombing.

Finally, for the night of 25 to 26 December, an area south of Tel Nof was bombed at 2330.

DAY 4
26 DECEMBER 1948

HOREV main effort forces advanced during the night of 25 to 26 December and attacked from the morning of Day 4; the weather improved and ILAF activity intensified, especially after sunrise at 0510.

FROM MIDNIGHT TO DAWN

0320–0550	103	1401	Katz Keidar Kenny Pozkanzner attack Faluja with 16*A100+AI3 bombs
0342–0450	106	RX-133/1704	Keren attack Gaza with 20*50+16*10kg bombs
0410–0440	3	0405	Dankner attack Faluja with 9*3kg incendiaries
0415–0610	103	Dalet172	Berliand Gochen attack Auja with 4*100lb bombs

The ILAF continued to harass Gaza (where the Egyptian main front HQ was reportedly based), Faluja (which the ILDF planned to attack in line with the ILPM's suggestion) and Auja, which was the prime target for the HOREV main effort. Squadron 106 C-46 raided Gaza from 0401 until 0410, as ILAFI reported:

Visibility was poor. On the first run, ten 50[kg bombs] and seven A/P bombs were dropped across center of town. Two

ILAF maintainers prepare a Beaufighter for a sortie; 26 December 1948 was the last ILAF Beaufighter mission.

Squadron 103 pilot George Berliand (left) flew ILAF Beaufighter's final mission on 26 December 1948; Berliand was photographed at Ramat David along with three Squadron 69 servicemen, left to right: gunner Jack Gershaw, gunner Harry Gershenson and navigator John Harris; crude conditions at Ramat David are plainly visible.

> fires were observed, one in vicinity of vehicles park and one in army camp. Both fires were bright yellow. On the second run, ten 50[kg bombs] and nine A/P bombs were dropped and hits were observed across center of town. It is possible that the hospital was hit. One large fire was observed after the second run. Medium ack ack was encountered and six searchlights were observed on south side of town; two on north-east side of town.

In bombing Faluja, it was planned that a Piper would mark the target with incendiaries ahead of the attack by Squadron 103. However, the C-47 crew reported that it was not notified that the target would be marked and it is possible that the C-47 actually attacked before the Piper that was over the target from 0425 until 0429, as ILAFI reported:

> Visibility was good. On first run over target, north-west to south-east, four bombs were dropped north of town. On the second run over target, north-west/south-east, five bombs were dropped north of town. Apparently, Squadron 103 C-47 arrived before Piper. About seven minutes' flying time from target, bombs were seen falling in the south.

The Squadron 103 C-47 was over Faluja, or more accurately looking for the target, from 0410 until 0511, as indicated in the debrief report:

> ... due to poor lighting and inefficient briefing (were not notified of Piper dropping incendiaries), could not identify target. Knew locality but due to presence of our troops in very near vicinity had to be extremely cautious... Dropped one box of incendiaries but bomb chuckers said box blew apart and almost lit tail. Dropped no more incendiaries!!! Came in north-east/south-west. Jettisoned bombs [from 5,000 feet] in dive, dropping at south-east section of perimeter as aiming point. Bombs assumed by pilot to have hit from center of town to southern section.

There was no need for target-marking of Auja because the Squadron 103 Beaufighter attacked at sunrise, from 0510 to 0515, in good weather and average visibility, as indicated in the debrief report:

> Run [heading 050] over large enemy concentration divided into two camps... Attacked southern camp... In camp, armored cars, trucks, troops and tents. Scored hits [during strafing] on tents... men and demolished three trucks... Target; run [heading] 230, east to west. Dropped all bombs. Missed given target due to intercom failure but straddled big houses... Incendiaries dropped on ground three yards off houses... On return had no radio and received no signals whatsoever from control. Pilot was unhappy as there was something definitely wrong with aircraft.

RAID AUJA

0520–0650	2	Piper	Rubens	attack Abu Ageila with 8*18kg bombs
0520–06:50	2	Piper	Solarsh	ditto
0520–0650	2	Piper	Portugali	ditto
0602–	106	RX-138 /1708	Moonitz Schild	VELVETTA 2, Tel Nof Niksic
0610–0735	35	1106	Gibson	attack Auja with 8*50kg bombs
0610–0735	35	1104	Kaplansky	ditto
0610–0638	35	1102	Soltau	ditto
0610–0735	35	1105	Flint	ditto
0615–1000	2		Piper	observation Bir Asluj Auja
0620–0745	101	2002/11	Augarten	escort Flight 35
0620–0745	101	2004/14	Senior	ditto

The ILDF was still advancing in the direction of Auja when Squadron 2 Pipers attacked Abu Ageila, some 20 kilometers west of Auja, and Flight 35 raided Auja. Squadron 2 Pipers attacked Abu Ageila from 0606 until 0645, as ILAFI reported:

> The first plane made four runs, dropping two bombs each time. The first two fell east of the camp of buildings. The second run bombs landed on the road in the middle of the camp. The next two runs were made over the tent camp and the bombs fell to the east of the camp.
> The second plane also made four runs. On the first run, two bombs were dropped which hit the west end of the camp of buildings. No hits were observed but the bombs fell close to the buildings. On the second run, two bombs were also dropped and the bombs fell on the north-east end of the buildings. On the third run, two bombs were dropped on the tent camp. No hits were observed. On the fourth run, two bombs were

DAY 4: 26 DECEMBER 1948

Squadron 2 Pipers raided Abu Ageila on the morning of 26 December 1948, dropping eight bombs each; the Pipers were modified with one quadruple bomb rack under the fuselage just behind the undercarriage and two double bomb racks on both sides of the fuselage just behind the struts; the depicted Squadron 2 Piper is possibly Alef52/0403.

A stick of at least 12 bombs, therefore dropped from a Squadron 69 B-17, over typical HOREV terrain.

dropped on the tent camp. Both bombs hit the south-east edge of the tent camp. All bombs exploded.

The third plane made three runs. On the first run, four bombs fell on the north-west side of the camp near the road between the tents. On the second run, two bombs were dropped on the slope of the wadi near the bridge on the side of the village. On the third run, two bombs were dropped among the houses of the village. A convoy of 15 trucks was observed in the village but this was apparently not hit. Direct hits were not observed but all bombs exploded.

Several of our armored vehicles were sighted around captured positions on the Bir Asluj/Auja road... Observed bombs falling in wadi to the north of Auja dropped by two T-6s. Thick smoke was seen from Auja. A Beaufighter was observed as circling near Auja... The road between Abu Ageila and Auja was observed as empty... At 0620... on the road Auja/Rafah... no cars were observed.

Flight 35 raided Auja from 0701 until 0706; three T-6s actually attacked, since the bombs of 1102 were dropped from the aircraft a short while after take-off, south-west of Faluja, due to a fault in switches, but no explosions were heard. ILAFI reported:

Eight bombs were released, two at a time, and hits were observed close to buildings. Eight bombs were released, four at a time, and hits were observed in other areas. Eight bombs were released at once; bombs overshot target about 300 yards to north-east and hit abandoned railway line.

Squadron 101 Spitfire pilots also monitored the Flight 35 raid, as ILAFI reported:

Visibility was unlimited. Observed two bombs fall in the courtyard of the police station about 25 yards from the building and two in the courtyard of the building next to the police station. Also observed three direct hits on the obsolete railway tracks north of Auja/Rafah junction and one south of the road near the junction.

Overall, Front D HQ reported that the bombing of Auja was effective. Also supporting HOREV forces advancing in the direction of Auja was the Squadron 2 Piper that took off at 0615, as ILAFI reported:

The area covered by this mission was Bir Asluj [to] Auja. Observed 22 vehicles... This position was shelled by our artillery and several vehicles were hit and destroyed while the remainder attempted to get away to the north. The enemy did not return fire.

RAID EL ARISH

0627–0833	69	1603	Katz Ben Porat Bresslof Weissbrod Kahn Ber Swiel Spicehandler Jacobson	attack El Arish with 36*100lb bombs
0630–0835	69	1602	Feldman Ratushniak Jacobs Michel Fink Lowenberg Soltan Nash Jackson Lazarus Joffe	attack El Arish with 30*A50 bombs
0630–0800	2	Piper	Halivni	observation Bir Asluj
0630–0800	2	Piper	Ospovat	observation Auja
0639–0806	101	2302/41	Weizman	escort Squadron 69
0649–0806	101	2003/12	Cohen	ditto

HOREV was already well into Day 4 and no encounters with enemy aircraft were reported over the battlefields. The start of the HOREV main effort prompted the ILAF to attack El Arish air base again, in order to secure ILAF air superiority over the HOREV theater of operations. Squadron 69 B-17s bombed from 0741, from 15,000 feet. Heavy, inaccurate AAA was encountered. The Feldman crew stated in the debrief report:

Crew observed no enemy aircraft on field or revetments. Field appears deserted but for AAA.

The debriefing officer added, at the bottom of the Katz crew debrief report form:

It is my opinion that, keeping in mind recent debriefings, the field is used as a decoy for our bombs.

Squadron 101 fighter pilots' impressions were indicated in an ILAFI report:

Visibility was very good. Observed the bombs fall south-east of intersection of runways. There is some doubt whether the last bomb fell on runway or not. Intense, heavy and very accurate ack ack was encountered from El Arish. This ack ack is considered the most accurate encountered as yet.

OBSERVATIONS

0703–0718	3	0110	Moller	Tel Nof Dov Field
0710–1025	2	Piper		observation Bir Asluj Auja
0715–0830	1	0702	Efrat	Dov Field Ramat David Dov Field
0743–0812	3	0405	Simantov	training
0800–0845	2	Piper	Biran	training
0805–1130	2	Piper		observation
0830–1300	2	Piper	Cohen	observation
0847–0900	3	0405	Dougherty	TelNof DovField
0937–1114	3	0409	Navot	observation Judea
0939–0958	3	0106	Giladi	Dov Field Tel Nof
0956–1015	3	0405	Goldstein	Dov Field Tel Nof
1000–1015	35	1103	Brown	Tel Nof Dov Field

The ILAF did not dispatch attack missions from 0630 until 1525 but continued to monitor the situation at Auja, while Squadron 3 pilot Nathan Navot flew observation east of Faluja, as ILAFI reported:

> Aircraft first recced road Beit Jibrin/Tarqumiya, where no movement was observed. On Tarqumiya/Hebron road... about four tents and two armored cars were observed... a small number of vehicles were observed traveling in both directions. On Hebron/Beer Sheba road there were also a few vehicles traveling in both directions. On the road from Dura... to the Beer Sheba road... a Grade B road which is fit for transport movement, a small car was seen moving towards Dura. At... road to Yatta... no movement was seen; the road appears to be in good condition. At Dahariya, near the police station, a gathering of people was observed; soldiers? The big building east of Shahiriya... appears to be a center; HQ or stores; guards and also a transport concentration were observed near it. In the southern sector of Dahariya village, a house with armored cars, trucks and small cars near it were observed. From Dahariya to the bombed bridge... about seven road blocks were observed. On the heights on both sides of the road there are entrenchments. The vicinity of Dahariya is full of Bedouin tents. At Dawayima... nothing new was observed. In the vicinity of Faluja Pocket airfield, artillery fire was observed – AAA? Single fire was encountered over Tarqumiya, Hebron and Dahariya – rifles?

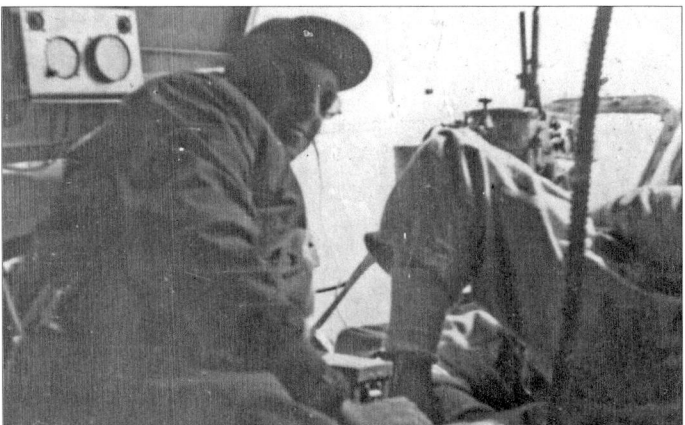

Hans Weissbrod, in the bombardier station of a Squadron 69 B-17, served in the RAF from 1940 until 1946. The German-born navigator-bombardier saw action with SAAF Squadron 34 that flew Wellington bombers from Italy. Weissbrod flew 42 missions from 15 July 1948 until 7 January 1949 and was lead bombardier on the 26 December 1948 morning mission to El Arish - a mission that generated concerns, as though bombing El Arish was a waste of effort.

VELVETTA 2 FLIGHT 2 DEPARTURE

1018–1618	106	RX-137/1707	Applebaum Styrack

VELVETTA 2 NIKSIC TEL NOF LEAD SHIP

1020–1610	101	2014	Cohen	VELVETTA 2 Niksic Tel Nof
1020–1610	101	2017	Blau	VELVETTA 2 Niksic Tel Nof
1020–1610	101	2018	Marmelstein	VELVETTA 2 Niksic Tel Nof
1023–1610	101	2010	Sinclair	VELVETTA 2 Niksic Tel Nof
1023–1610	101	2013	Ruch	VELVETTA 2 Niksic Tel Nof
1023–1610	101	2016	Finkel	VELVETTA 2 Niksic Tel Nof

None of the Operation VELVETTA 2 flight 1 Spitfires had flown in Israel – and, in any case, Squadron 101 fighters were not yet hard-pressed due to the absence of EGAF fighters from HOREV theater of operations – by the time Operation VELVETTA 2 flight 2 Spitfires departed Yugoslavia.

Squadron 3 pilot Nathan Navot flew Piper 0409 to monitor activity at the Judea sector on 26 December 1948; Piper 0409 is equipped with racks for eight bombs: four under the fuselage just behind the undercarriage and two each side of the fuselage.

LATE MORNING TO MIDDAY

1044–1103	3	0106	Front	training
1045–1100	1	0114	Kahana	training
1050–1150	2	Piper	Zibel	training
1054–1229	101	2004/14	Feldman	patrol Auja Rafah
1054–1229	101	2302/41	Goodlin	ditto
1100–1200	2	Piper	Eyal	training
1100–1300	2	Piper	Solarsh	observation Bir Asluj
1110–1605	1	1305	Efrat	Dov Field Hatzor Dov Field StJean Ramat David Tel Nof Dov Field
1135–1330	1	0702	Kaplan	Dov Field Ramat David Dov Field
11 50–1210	1	0114	Steinman Kahana	Dov Field Tel Nof

Squadron 1 Rapides were not used for bombing during HOREV even though, at the same time, bombing tests were flown in Rapide 1302.

Squadron 101 pilots, at Hatzor, in front of S199 1906, during the winter of 1948 to 1949. Left to right: Slick Goodlin, Aaron Finkel and Syd Cohen; Syd Cohen was Squadron 101 Commander from 3 November 1948.

1150–1230	3	0409	Simantov	training
1155–1300	101	Piper	Axelrod	Hatzor Tel Nof Hatzor
1200–1320	1	1302	Renov	test bombing

ILAF's monitoring of HOREV thereater of operations continued with a Squadron 101 pair – a Spitfire and a P-51, the combination due to the small number of available fighters coupled with low serviceability – and a Squadron 2 Piper, but EGDF activity was minor and EGAF activity was practically nil. ILAFI reported:

> Flew over road south of Bir Asluj, highway east of Auja, Auja/Suez Canal road and Auja/Rafah road. Observed little movement on these various roads.

OBSERVATION AUJA

1202–1646	106	RX-136 /1709	Krokstedt	VELVETTA 2 search and rescue
1300–1518	3	0409	Goldstein	Tel Nof Beer Sheba Tel Nof
1310–1400	101	2001/10	Cohen	photo Gaza Rafah
1310–1400	101	1906	(Augarten)	photo Gaza Rafah escort
1315–1720	1	0602	Machnes	Dov Field Haifa Dov Field
1343–1652	3	0114	Navot	Tel Nof Dov Field Tel Nof
1345–1635	1	1306	Lahat	Dov Field Hatzor Beer Sheba Dov Field
1402–1549	3	0106	Giladi	observation Faluja
1425–1710	2	0402	(Zibel)	observation Auja
1445–1700	2	0403	(Portugali)	observation
1508–1918	103	1403	Katz Agmon Millman	Ramat David Tel Nof Sodom Tel Nof

Squadron 101's photo of Rafah was abortive due to camera malfunction; but the pilots reported observation of 30 to 40 vehicles, and several tents, in a dispersal roughly a kilometer south of town.

Squadron 2 and Squadron 3 continued to monitor Auja and Faluja, respectively. There was nothing new over Faluja, while 0402 was tasked to evaluate EGDF deployment in the Auja sector in preparation for an ILDF attack against Auja. ILAFI reported:

> The plane flew west to a distance of about 10 kilometers from Auja along Auja/Rafah road in order to inspect whether there were any enemy forces on the road and the direction of their movement. A group of about 20 trucks was observed moving towards Auja, on the road, about 10 kilometers west of Auja. From there inspected the road in the direction of Auja. In vicinity of Auja, the enemy occupies positions on dominating heights. Then recced the Auja/Ismailia road in the Auja/Abu Ageila sector. In this sector, a number of vehicles were seen traveling towards Egypt. From there, the aircraft returned to Auja/Rafah road. Observed a group of enemy armored cars, which encountered our forces and a fight ensued. A note was dropped by the aircraft to the local forces who were in the area regarding this fight.

RAID RAFAH

1525–1707	69	1603	Raisin Ratushniak Harris Cuburnek attack Rafah with 29*D70 bombs Lichtman Duboff Aronson Meyerson Kaplan Gershaw Joffe
1526–1703	69	1602	McConville Noach Seftel Weinstein attack Rafah with 28*D70 bombs Christiensen Kahn Schwartzbach Cohen Robinson Cohen Liponetzky Lazarus

The ILDF intended to renew its HOREV secondary effort during the night of 26 to 27 December as a diversion to the impending attack against Auja, so the ILAF was tasked to harass Egyptian forces in the sector of secondary effort as well as to pin down Egyptian forces so that the Auja sector would not be reinforced. The B-17s flew unescorted along the coastline and bombed from 1616, from 16,000 feet. The wingman reported:

> Unidentified aircraft (fighter type) followed kites from Gaza Majdal... at 4,000 [meters] distance; same place (Gaza) where planes seen yesterday.

The bombing was not considered a success. Lead bombardier Cuburnek reported:

> All bombs considerably overshot.

Wingman navigator Seftel added:

> Missed given target. Believe that some damage done to some dumps.

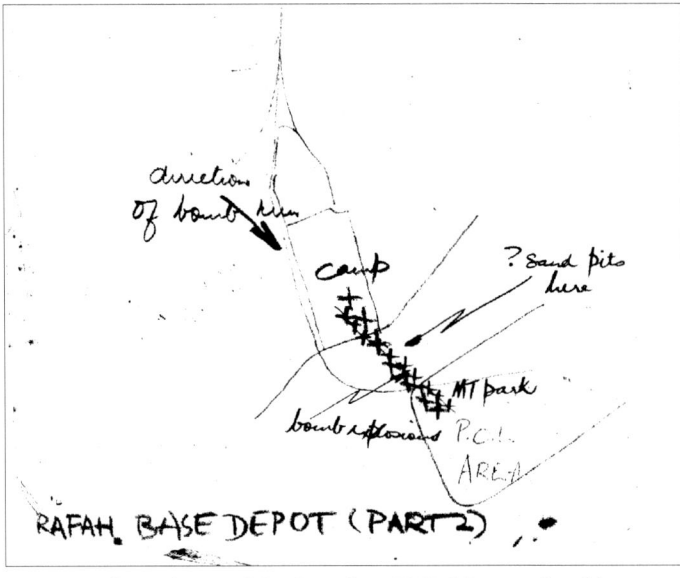

The debriefing scheme of the Squadron 69 Rafah camp bombing mission on the afternoon of 26 December 1948.

Flight 35 T-6 1103 was damaged in a landing accident on 26 December 1948 when flown by Grisha Brown; 1103 - which did not fly a single HOREV mission until the accident - was duly repaired but returned to fly only after the end of HOREV.

END OF DAY 4

1540–1550	1	0603	Renov	test
1600–1700	2	0408	Biran	observation Faluja
1605–1755	1	0603	Renov	Dov Field Ramat David Dov Field
1632–1659	3	0409	Katzin	test
1639–1835	2	0404	Rubens	Beer Sheba Tel Nof Beer Sheba
1645–1706	3	0110)	Front	test
1645–2120	1	1305	Kaplan	Dov Field Tel Nof Haifa Ramat David Dov Field
1647–1705	3	0405	Ruff	Tel Nof Dov Field
1707–1725	35	1103	Brown	Dov Field Tel Nof, accident
1727–2045	103	1405	Orringer Wygle Festing Manor	attack Faluja with 16*100kg bombs
2109–2313	103	1403	Katz Agmon Millman	Tel Nof Sodom Tel Nof

Squadron 2 pilot Nahum Biran was tasked to look for a camel caravan that was, reportedly, on its way to the Faluja Pocket. Visibility was good but the caravan was not found.

1103 was damaged in a landing accident at Tel Nof; it was repaired but did not return to fly until after the end of Operation HOREV.

EGAF evening bombings continued with a raid against Lod/Lydda airport, as ILAFI reported:

> Rishon Le Zion and Petah Tikva reported a reddish rocket dropping slowly. This may have been a flare dropped by plane which bombed Lydda at 1836. Bomb fell east of airfield on old railway station. Six (?) bombs were thrown. Two bombs only exploded, fell between Sarafand and Lydda.

Squadron 103 1405 was to attack Faluja but instead bombed Gaza from 2015 until 2017, from 9,000 feet, as indicated in the debrief report:

> Over target [Faluja] at 18:30... Target not illuminated as briefed. Did square search for one hour. Returned [to Tel Nof as initial point] and attempted to track to Faluja again. Did square search for 15 minutes... All bombs dropped over Gaza... All bombs exploded... Three searchlights on the road from the sea to Gaza town.

An ILDF evening attack on Auja failed. The ILAF was unable to support the ILDF during night-time but bombed Auja only from 0510 until 0706, so too many hours passed from the end of ILAF raids until the start of the ILDF attack. In any case, the number of sorties that actually attacked Auja – only four – and the mass of bombs dropped on Auja – at best 1,380 kilograms – were too little to matter. At 2045, Front D HQ reported:

> - After our forces penetrated Auja, we were forced to retreat due to enemy concentrated anti-tank fire. We suffered some 25 casualties as well as a number of armored vehicles.
> - Enemy advanced some 25 armored vehicles from Rafah [to Auja, running into ILDF ambush]. We destroyed five and the balance is hiding in darkness.
> - We are making an effort to assemble our forces for a renewed attack [against Auja] at dawn.
> - All [ILAF] bombings should be directed to stop enemy movements in this sector and to engage Rafah.

DAY 5
27 DECEMBER 1948

ILDF's main objective during Day 5 was to occupy Auja and Bir Asluj, as well as to renew the Brigade 1 attack in the Rafah to Gaza sector, but deteriorating weather adversely impacted ILAF activity.

HARASS FALUJA

0113–0319	103	1401	Boshes Nathan Weinstein Kemp	attack Faluja with 16*A100 bombs
0256–0353	103	1405	Orringer Wygle Festing Manor	attack Faluja with 16*100lb bombs

Harassment of Faluja continued but at a rather low intensity, with only three C-47 raids from sunset on 26 December at 1647 until sunrise on 27 December sunrise at 0511. During this timeframe, the Squadron 1, Squadron 3 and Squadron 106 potential of 'night bombers' did not fly a single sortie.

Squadron 103's 1401 crew reported good weather. The C-47 was over the target from 0200 until 0237; an ILDF searchlight was

A staged photo - taken in October 1949 - illustrating mission planning during wartime. Left to right: ILAF Commander Aaron Remez, Operations Officer Smoky Simon, Operations Officer Shlomo Lahat (Squadron 1 Commander at the time of HOREV) and ILAF Photography Unit Commander Baruch Kris.

activated at Iraq Suidan in the direction of Faluja, yet the C-47 crew experienced difficulties in pinpointing the target due to the blackout and haze but finally bombed from 4,000 feet. ILAFI reported:

> The bombs were dropped in the north-west corner of Faluja. One big explosion and black smoke was seen. Light machine gun and occasional 20mm ack ack were encountered.

Squadron 103's C-147 1405 crew reported 10 to 15 miles visibility over target, was over target from 0308 until 0308 and bombed from 5,000 feet, as elaborated in its debrief report:

> Searchlight from Iraq Suidan as briefed. Bombs dropped... about 100 yards to port of searchlight beam, from north-west to south-east. Bombs believed to have dropped in north-west of town.

OBSERVATION AUJA

0645–0955	2	0403		observation Quseima Abu Ageila Auja
0659–0725	3	0110	Front	Tel Nof Dov Field
0720–1220	2	0408	(Zibel)	observation Auja

Squadron 2 0403 was tasked to monitor the whereabouts of Egyptian forces, as ILAFI reported:

> In Quseima... a concentration of about seven vehicles and troops was observed. On road from Quseima to Abu Ageila only a few vehicles were seen. In Abu Ageila about 25 to 30 trucks and other types of vehicles were seen scattered in the village area. There was no sign of entrenchments. In section of road between Auja and Abu Ageila, about nine kilometers from Abu Ageila, there is a concentration of about 70 vehicles of all types. About 15 of these vehicles were on the road traveling in the direction of Abu Ageila. There was no sign of entrenchments.

Squadron 2 0408 was tasked to monitor activity at Auja, and the surrounding sector, amidst the ILDF attack, as ILAFI reported:

Another staged photo from October 1949 replayed a Squadron 103 brief for a HOREV bombing mission; the briefing officer, Sam Boshes, flew 10 C-47 bombing missions during HOREV.

Approximately 10 armored cars were observed on Auja/Rafah road near intersection with stream Auja (west of the road); 40 more trucks were gathered about two kilometers west of the road. Shells were exploding among the armored cars.

ATTACK MANSHIYA

0800–0845	35	1106	Gibson	attack Manshiya with 8*50kg bombs
0800–0845	35	1101	Soltau	ditto
0800–0845	35	1104	Brown	ditto
0800–0845	35	1105	Flint	ditto
0800–0845	35	1107	Black	ditto

In line with the ILPM recommendation to eliminate the Faluja Pocket, the ILDF planned to launch Operation ELIMINATION during the night of 27 to 28 December 1948, with Brigade 3 attacking Iraq Manshiya - east of Faluja - with an objective to scale down the pocket, as the first phase of its total elimination. The ILAF was tasked to soften the sector of attack, but again – just like the night-time harassment effort – air raids were too few and too spaced to matter. ILAFI reported:

> Visibility was poor. Leading aircraft dropped his bombs four at a time, on one run, on north-west side of town. Second aircraft made two runs, dropping four bombs at a time; four of these fell on target (center) and four others on north-west edge of target. Third aircraft dropped his bombs two at a time and all exploded within the target area. Fourth aircraft dropped his bombs four at a time and observed them falling on target area. Fifth aircraft dropped his bombs four at a time on the same run; of these, three bombs fell short of target and four in the center. Explosions were clearly seen and many flashes were also observed across town from south-east to north-west... inaccurate ack ack was encountered.

DETERIORATING WEATHER

0900–1200	2	Piper	Eyal	observation
0925–0935	101	2002/11		
0925–0935	101	2004/14		
0940–1020	2	0408		observation BirAsluj
1005–1105	101	0419		Hatzor Dov Field Hatzor

1005–1520	1	1302	Ospovat		Dov Field Hatzor Tel Nof Dov Field
1100–1300	2	Piper	Biran		observation
1100–1300	2	Piper	Halivni		observation
1105–1210	101	0419			Hatzor Tel Nof Hatzor
1125–1235	1	0702	Machnes Avisar		training

Squadron 2 0408 was tasked to pinpoint the position of Egyptian forces reportedly retreating from Bir Asluj but was forced to abort its mission, as ILAFI reported:

> Reached Ruhama and did not proceed south due to low clouds and a strong side wind.

AUJA IN OUR HANDS

1130–1215	101	2002/11	Feldman		scramble to Auja
1130–1230	101	2004/14	Weizman		ditto
1130–1230	101	2302/41	Goodlin		ditto

Front D reported, at 1135, that Auja was in its hands. ILAFI Condensed Operational Summary Number 4 reported:

> Heavy fighting raged around Auja during the night of 26 to 27 December 1948. Rain hampered activities in the morning but by 1140 the town was completely in our hands. Our forces have cut both roads leading from Auja westward; the one to Rafah and the other to Abu Ageila.

The fall of Auja possibly prompted the first ILDF-reported appearance of EGAF fighters over the battlefields since start of HOREV, so Squadron 101 fighters were scrambled to Auja. Squadron 101 pilot Seymour Feldman reported poor visibility and the first sighting of enemy fighters over HOREV battlefields, as indicated in his debrief:

> Proceeded to Auja and observed a FIAT flying south of Auja. Spitfire chased the FIAT (who headed south) but could not catch him. Then returned to base.

Weizman and Goodlin, in a P-51 and Spitfire, also headed to Auja, as ILAFI reported:

> Visibility was fair. Observed approximately 20 trucks and at least 10 tanks... on El Arish/Auja road. Made a pass at two tanks and a... truck. Observed strikes on all of them. Observed... 150 to 200 men on a hill... and entrenchments. Then strafed a... truck (stationary)... At... observed a concentration of vehicles and tanks and strafed two tanks which were standing... alone. Observed strikes on both of them and later observed white smoke arising from there. The Spitfire then proceeded to base, and approximately five miles south of Gaza made a pass on a truck on the highway. After the Spitfire hit the two tanks mentioned above, the Mustang circled target area and made a pass at a concentration of vehicles... with unknown results.

ASLUJ APPEARS EMPTY

1155–1705	1	1305	Kaplan		Dov Field Haifa Ramat David Haifa Ramat David Tel Nof Dov Field

The first ILAF indication of EGAF fighters flying over the battlefield surfaced on 27 December 1948; in this image an EGAF Spitfire is flying over rooftops during HOREV.

Squadron 1 operated Rapides, Bonanzas, Norecrins and Pipers that were mostly tasked to fly liaison and transport missions during HOREV; three of Squadron 1's aircraft were also configured for CASEVAC including the two Norecrins, one of which was photographed during the CASEVAC demo.

1158–1241	3	0106	Biram		training
1300–1345	101	2008/15			test
1310–1535	1	0702	Machnes		Dov Field Beer Sheba Dov Field
1354–1705	3	0106	Moller		Tel Nof Beer Sheba Hatzor Tel Nof
1400–1445	101	0419			Hatzor Dov Field Hatzor
1400–1655	1	0603	Renov		Dov Field Ramat David Haifa Ramat David Dov Field
1430–1650	2	0403			observation Gaza Rafah
1433–1608	3	0114	Navot		Tel Nof Dov Field Tel Nof
1500–1700	2	Piper	Portugali		observation Bir Asluj
1515–1635	101	2004/14	Cohen)		patrol Auja
1515–1645	101	2302/41	Doyle		patrol Auja
1535–1705	2	0408	(Portugali)		observation Bir Asluj
1545–1615	101	2301/40			test
1545–1625	101	0419			Hatzor Tel Nof Hatzor

The first thus far unearthed flight of a VELVETTA 2 Spitfire from an ILAF air base was accomplished from 1300 when 2008 departed Hatzor for a test. Squadron 101 was dispatched to the Faluja sector, at 1515, another armed patrol, as ILAFI reported:

Visibility was poor. Observed at least 40 vehicles (including armored cars and tanks) traveling east... Observed a long convoy traveling north towards Rafah. Observed Egyptian markings on these vehicles. Strafed a wireless truck... a truck with a tank on it, an armored car (definitely damaged) and then a large truck (unidentified as ambulance until pilot flew over). A burst of ack ack was encountered in the Auja area.

Squadron 2 0408 was tasked to inspect Bir Asluj, as ILAFI reported:

Asluj appears to be empty of people and deserted.

RAID MANSHIYA

1558–1626	35	1106	Gibson	attack Manshiya with 8*50kg bombs
1558–1626	35	1101	Brown	ditto
1558–1626	35	1102	Soltau	ditto
1558–1626	35	1104	Kaplansky	ditto
1558–1626	35	1105	Flint	ditto
1558–1626	35	1107	Black	ditto

Flight 35 returned to Iraq Manshiya for a second raid during Day 5 and the final raid prior to Brigade 3's attack, as ILAFI reported:

Visibility over target was poor to fair. Leading aircraft dropped all bombs carried on it, two at a time on one run; all fell into target area and were seen exploding. Second plane made four runs over target; three bomb runs and the fourth strafing; on the first run, four bombs were dropped in center of town – all of these exploded; on the second run, two bombs were dropped – the bombs exploded 100 meters from top of hill north of town, bombs hit east side of hill; on the third run, two bombs were dropped west of hilltop and all exploded; on the fourth run, the aircraft strafed hill, road and town. Third aircraft released eight bombs over north-west part of town; they drifted from there to center of town. Fourth plane dropped four bombs, which were seen hitting the ground about 100 feet from the base of the hill, and the second lot of four bombs dropped by this aircraft hit the base of the hill. All eight bombs of the fifth aircraft hit the target. The eight bombs of the sixth aircraft were observed hitting the east side of the hill. Light machine-gun fire was encountered by one of the aircraft and one flash

was encountered by another aircraft between Faluja and Iraq Manshiya.

END OF DAY 5

1620 –	1	1301	Ospovat	Dov Field Beer Sheba Dov Field
1630–1845	101	0419		Hatzor Dov Field Tel Nof Hatzor
1740–1905	103	1401	Rosin Agmon Kenny Boettger attack Faluja with 16*A100 bombs	
2100–0802	3	0405	Biram	Tel Nof Dov Field Beer Sheba Tel Nof
2400–0320	1	1301	Machnes	Dov Field Beer Sheba Dov Field

Front D reported, at 1800, that Bir Asluj was in Israeli hands, along with the whole Auja sector. ILAFI Condensed Operational Summary Number 4 added:

At 1800 it is reported that Bir Asluj has been captured together with the heights surrounding the town. The enemy succeeded in withdrawing its forces from Bir Asluj and has transferred them to Abu Ageila.

Brigade 3 initiated Operation ELIMINATION with an attack against Iraq Manshiya, but the ILAF dispatched only a single sortie, tasked to bomb Faluja, from sunset at 1647 on 27 December until sunrise at 0511 on 28 December. Squadron 103's 1401 crew was over Faluja from 1829 until 1847; the crew reported good weather, described visibility as very dark and bombed from 3,000 feet in the face of no AAA fire, as indicated in its debrief:

Our bombing run direction [was] 100 [degrees]... Bombs straddled through center of town, just south of new road to Manshiya in northern edge of build-up area and parallel to road. Normal bomb explosions. No fires observed.

The 1401 crew complained that the promised ILDF searchlight, to mark the target, was not active, that the communication code was inadequate and that Israel was not wholly blacked out, especially along the Haifa to Tel Aviv road. Upon completion of bombing, the 1401 crew landed at Tel Nof.

Squadron 1 Norecrins and a Rapide had been modified as air ambulances; the first thus far unearthed Squadron 1 CASEVAC mission in a Norecrin or a Rapide, during HOREV, was when Benjamin Machnes departed Dov Field at midnight and returned from Beer Sheba with four casualties.

Day 5 ended positively for the ILDF. ILAFI Condensed Operational Summary Number 4 reported that the only detected enemy air activity from 1900 on 26 December until 1900 on 27 December was the bombing of Jura, north of Gaza, with two bombs that did no damage. ILAFI Condensed Operational Summary Number 5 summed up:

The Beer Sheba/Bir Asluj/Auja road is completely in our hands. It is being used to bring up reinforcements and supplies to our forces in the southern sector.
The summary of fighting on 27 December indicated that we took 200 to 250 captives in the Auja area. The bag includes several officers, including a Lieutenant Colonel.

The ILAF inventory included eight T-6s, but 1108 did not fly during HOREV and 1103 did not fly attack missions during HOREV, so the actual maximum T-6 force was six aircraft, as flown during the Day 5 afternoon mission to raid Manshiya.

Squadron 69 and Squadron 103 operated B-17s (left) and C-47s (right) from Ramat David during HOREV with Squadron 69 B-17s flying daytime bombings and Squadron 103 C-47s flying night-time bombings.

In the Bir Asluj area, the enemy successfully withdrew his forces but left behind a portion of his equipment. This includes three 6pounders (anti-tank guns), six 3-inch mortars and six machine guns.
Interrogation of officers taken prisoner reveals that the Egyptians expected the main Israeli attack on the western sector (Gaza Rafah area) and underestimated the strength of our forces in the southern [Auja] sector.

But all of this positive impression – from an Israeli perspective – was to change by the morning of Day 6.

DAY 6
28 DECEMBER 1948

HOREV's offensive against Auja and Bir Asluj, during Day 5, was wholly successful, but Operation ELIMINATION, launched during the night of 27 to 28 December, ran into troubles during the morning of Day 6.

AIR COMBAT FROM FALUJA TO RAFAH

0510–0930	1	1301	Solarsh	Dov Field Beer Sheba Dov Field
0630–0830	2	Piper	Biran	observation Bir Asluj
0630–0900	2	Piper	Portugali	observation Auja
0640–0930	2	0401)	Eyal	observation Auja Rafah Khan Yunes
0705–1624	3	0114	Giladi	Tel Nof Dov Field Tel Nof
0715–0825	101	2002/11	Doyle	escort Flight 35
0720–0820	101	2001/10	Levett	escort Flight 35
0720–0809	3	0409	Simantov	training

Squadron 2 pilot Eli Eyal was tasked to look for a soft spot in the EGDF deployment as Front D was looking for options to exploit the success of Auja's occupation. ILAFI reported:

> Visibility was bad. The object of the recce was a recce of enemy positions and fortifications, and a search for a spot which will enable a breakthrough. As visibility was bad, nothing was observed.

Squadron 3 pilot Aaron Biram, returning to Tel Nof from Beer Sheba in 0405, sighted enemy aircraft, as ILAFI reported:

An Egyptian Macchi - EGAF Number 1214 - at a Suez Canal Zone airfield during HOREV; ILAF was aware that Egypt acquired Italian fighters - both FIAT and Macchi - and referred to all encountered Egyptian Italian fighters as FIAT.

An Egyptian FIAT - EGAF Number 1260 - photographed during HOREV. Unknown to ILAF at the time, EGAF actually utilized Macchi more than FIAT during HOREV.

> Before reaching Ruhama, observed four aircraft flying in a north-east/south-west direction. The aircraft returned when our aircraft reached Ruhama and passed our aircraft. Observed bombs falling between Jamama and Ruhama. Observed dogfight between possibly one or more of our aircraft... and the enemy aircraft. Contacted Tel Aviv... The construction of the enemy aircraft lead to the belief that there were... Furies among them and the insignia seen on the tail was a rectangle with three rectangular stripes of red, white and blue. Owing to fact that aircraft passed by very quickly, this is not certain.

This seems to be a quite confused report. The proper timeline of events may have been a sighting of enemy aircraft that attacked Ruhama sector, a radio report to Tel Aviv and then a sighting of the dogfight. Rudy Augarten reported in the Squadron 101 debrief:

Just as planes were taking off on mission, enemy planes were sighted over Faluja. Our flight intercepted bandits initially off the coast at Majdal. There was one Spit and four or five FIATs. The ensuing dogfight ranged down to the area south-west of Rafah. Levett observed strikes on two aircraft. Doyle observed strikes also on two aircraft, one of which was burning. In the opinion of Doyle and Levett, the FIAT is extremely maneuverable and definitely faster than our pointed-wing Spits. When intercepted, bandits were in a gaggle and at least two were firing at our flight but hit nothing.

Doyle wrote in his logbook:

Jumped eight FIATs; I destroyed one [and] damaged one; Levett damaged two.

While ILAFI reported:

Six planes were observed in a dogfight near Faluja. One plane fell into the sea.

A narrative attempting to present an Arab perspective of this engagement can be described as ranging from inaccurate to twisted:

On 28 December... [Egypt] claimed the downing of two Israeli aircraft, with two others damaged, for the loss of one Egyptian machine... while an Israeli Avia [S199] fighter was seriously damaged in a large air battle over the Faluja Pocket. The Egyptian loss was a Macchi flown by... Abed Fatah Said who was killed by... Doyle flying a Spitfire during... air strike against the dispersal strip at Abu Ageila on 28 December... a dogfight involving many aircraft developed over Faluja... this time the outcome was more balanced and may even have been to the Egyptian pilots' advantage. The Israelis claimed to have shot down one [EGAF] Spitfire although the only Egyptian aircraft reported lost on 28 December was a Macchi over Abu Ageila... An... [ILAF] Avia... [S199] also fell away from Faluja trailing smoke. This may have been the aircraft... which Israeli sources unofficially admitted losing... without supplying a precise date. [PXNE, p115–17]

Not a single ILAF S199 sortie was flown on 28 December and none of the two Squadron 101 Spitfires engaged in combat on the morning of 28 December was hit, regardless of what was written many years later. The combination of the two prominent facts – the ILDF sighting of a fighter crashing into the Mediterranean Sea and Egyptian admission of a Macchi loss – suggests that the 28 December morning air combat resulted in a single kill, most likely the one attributed to Doyle.

Embarrassingly, the Israeli side also seems to have inflated the combat outcome as the ILAF credited not one but three kills: Levett was credited with a FIAT kill and a Spitfire kill; Doyle was credited with a Macchi kill.

RAID FALUJA

0750–0815	35	1106	Gibson	attack Faluja with 8*50kg bombs
0750–0815	35	1101	Brown	ditto
0750–0815	35	1102	Soltau	ditto
0750–0815	35	1104	Kaplansky	ditto
0750–0815	35	1105	Flint	ditto
0750–0815	35	1107	Black	ditto

ELIMINATION's Brigade 3 attack against Iraq Manshiya met stiff resistance and determined counter-attack, so Brigade 3, at 0500, requested massive ILAF support from sunrise at 0637. Flight 35 attacked Faluja from 0804, under the cover of Squadron 101 pilots Doyle and Levett, who returned to Faluja, after the end of air combat, and reported that all bombs hit Faluja. ILAFI elaborated:

Visibility was cloudy. Four bombs were observed hitting 100 feet north-east from gun positions. Two aircraft had to make a second run each in order to release bombs which had been hung up. Hits from all six aircraft were observed surrounding gun positions, but no direct hits were observed; 20mm ack ack was encountered.

While fighting in the Faluja Pocket continued, ILPM David Ben-Gurion met with Front B Commander Shlomo Shamir and emphasized the importance of this battle:

We will not be drawn to battle in Front B sector against our will. Fall of Faluja may seal the fate of Gaza. After the end of the offensive in the south, we will evaluate the situation, whether to attack or not to attack in the Front B sector.

However, the ILDF and ILAF failed to pin down Egyptian forces in the Faluja Pocket; the EGDF counter-attacked and forced Brigade 3 to retreat from Iraq Manshiya. ELIMINATION failed; but HOREV continued.

ELIMINATION RETREAT

0905–0948	3	0106	Front	training
0910–1130	1	0702	Efrat	Dov Field St Jean Ramat David Dov Field
0912–0942	3	0110	Sutton	training
0915–1545	106	RX-131	BenSimon	VELVETTA 2 Niksic Tel Nof
0932–1000	35	1106	Gibson	attack Faluja with 8*50kg bombs
0932–1000	35	1101	Brown	ditto
0932–1000	35	1102	Soltau	ditto
0932–1000	35	1104	Kaplansky	ditto
0932–1000	35	1105	Flint	ditto
0932–1000	35	1107	Black	ditto

Instead of a massive softening of the Faluja Pocket prior to Operation ELIMINATION, and after Egyptian forces were not pinned down during Operation ELIMINATION's morning battle at Iraq Manshiya, the ILAF initiated a massive attack against the Faluja Pocket, primarily because Operation ELIMINATION failed – with Brigade 3 losing more than 90 killed soldiers. The ILDF feared that Egyptian forces in the Faluja Pocket might attempt to exploit its success for a breakthrough from the blockade; an action that would have jeopardized all of HOREV's accomplishments. Flight 35 was back over the Faluja Pocket from 0950 until 0951, as ILAFI reported:

Flying School cadet Eli Eyal was assigned to Squadron 1 when the ILAF suspended Flying School training in preparation for HOREV; ILAF Adjutancy reported, on 27 December 1948, that Eyal was reassigned from Squadron 1 to Squadron 2 - a unit he commanded in early 1948 prior to assignment to the Flying School by mid-1948 - from 24 December 1948 and on 28 December 1948 Eli Eyal flew observation sorties to find a breakthrough point in enemy deployment.

Flight 35 T-6 1105 - photographed flying in 1949 - flew 18 missions during HOREV; Flight 35 pilot Mitchell Flint flew at least 15 missions in 1105 during HOREV.

Visibility was good... Two direct hits on the road [from Faluja to Iraq Manshiya] were observed and the remainder on either side. Bombs dropped by the following aircraft were observed to score a hit or near miss on vehicles, hits or near misses on the bridge, hits and explosions on either side of the road; 40mm ack ack was encountered over Iraq Manshiya.

VELVETTA 2 OPERATIONAL DEBUT

Time	Sqn	A/C	Pilot	Mission
0935–1010	2	0401	(Eyal)	observation
0945–1105	101	0419	Axelrod	Hatzor TelN of Hatzor
0950–1105	101	2008/15	Weizman	escort Flight 35
0950–1105	101	2302/41	Senior	ditto
1005–1010	101	2301/40		test
1015–1150	1	0603	Ospovat	Dov Field Ramat David Dov Field
1025–1140	2	0401	Eyal	observation
1035–1315	1	1301	Kaplan	Dov Field Beer Sheba Dov Field
1100–1454	3	0106	Front	Tel Nof Ramat David Tel Nof
1111–1137	101	2012/16	Feldman	test, delivery Tel Nof Hatzor
1115–1425	1	1306	Renov	Dov Field Tel Nof Beer Sheba Dov Field

The first thus far unearthed VELVETTA 2 Spitfire to fly a Squadron 101 operation is 2008, which flew, from 0950 until 1105, a mission to escort Flight 35 to attack Faluja, but the Flight 35 T-6s had already attacked from 0950 until 0951, as ILAFI reported:

Visibility over target was good. The fighters did not observe the Harvards drop their bombs. Escorted them to base and then patrolled the Faluja area. Nothing observed.

Squadron 2 pilot Eli Eyal continued to monitor the HOREV theater of operations, as ILAFI reported:

Visibility over target was good. The object of the mission was a recce of enemy positions and fortifications and a search for a possible breakthrough point. Also an observation of our ambush point... [along] Rafah/Auja road (20 kilometers from Rafah). West of Abasan... an orange grove with a concentration of tents, vehicles and troops was observed. Along Khan Yunes/Rafah road, about 200 meters east of the road, enemy trenches and fortifications were seen. Tents were also observed about 20 kilometers from Rafah Auja [and] Rafah El Arish crossroads. A destroyed Egyptian tank was observed on the side of the road, presumably an outcome of the mining of the road at night.

RAID FALUJA

Time	Sqn	A/C	Pilot	Mission
1120–1202	3	0405		observation Faluja
1125–1152	35	1106	Gibson	attack Faluja with 8*50kg bombs
1125–1152	35	1102	Soltau	ditto
1125–1152	35	1107	Black	ditto
1125–1152	35	1105	Flint	ditto
1125–1152	35	1104	Kaplansky	ditto
1125–1152	35	1101	Brown	ditto

Flight 35 raided Faluja, again, from 1140 until 1141, in two flights of three aircraft each. ILAFI reported the action of the first flight (1107, 1102 and 1106):

Hits were observed on the north-east base of the hill and up the side, overshot to base on south-west side, no direct hits were observed on top. The second and third aircraft took the main road into Manshiya to attack armored column. Observed direct hit and a large explosion on target and a few scattered hits on target area.

Second flight (1105, 1104 and 1101) flew one run, dropping all eight bombs at once and hitting the south-west side of Iraq Manshiya. Squadron 3 0405 monitored the Flight 35 attack, as ILAFI reported:

Visibility was good. Road from Faluja to Iraq Manshiya was recced and holes were seen on either sides of bridge... but the bridge was not touched. Three Harvard aircraft attacked

Squadron 101 pilot Rudy Augarten prepares for flight in a Spitfire; Augarten flew at least 16 sorties during HOREV, including nine in Spitfires and the balance in S199 and P-51.

concentrations north/north-west of Iraq Manshiya. The hill was attacked and a trench on the west side of the hill was observed to have been hit, and two hits were scored on the east side of the hill. At the crossroads of Iraq Manshiya road and the road turning north from Iraq Manshiya, an explosion followed immediately by a fire which died down quickly... The rest of the bombs were observed to fall in the vicinity.

1101 was damaged during landing and was grounded for repairs until 4 January 1949.

PATROL NORTH-EAST SINAI

1145–1255	101	2002/11	Augarten	patrol north-east Sinai
1145–1255	101	2004/14	Dangott	ditto
1200–1215	101	0419	(Axelrod)	training or Hatzor Tel Nof Hatzor

HOREV forces were still on hold, preparing for the next phase of the offensive. Operation ELIMINATION forces were reorganizing after a bloody retreat from the Faluja Pocket. It was during this timeframe that two Squadron 101 Spitfires were sent to patrol over north-east Sinai, as ILAFI reported:

> Visibility was good. A large fire or explosion among a group of buildings was observed one mile north-east of Rafah main sub-depot. Observed a train approximately 15 miles east of El Arish, heading towards El Arish, which consisted of a locomotive, two passenger cars and 12 box cars. Spitfires made four passes on it and observed strikes on locomotive and cars but did not see any fire or smoke. The train stopped... Then flew to reported airfield south of El Arish. The same three Spitfires were observed. More equipment was seen on the field and the place which was reported as being worked on (possibly another runway or ground being ploughed) was larger than when last seen. Observed a convoy of 18 vehicles traveling south on Gaza/Rafah highway and other scattered transport traveling in both directions. Also observed a small amount of traffic moving in both directions on El Arish/Auja highway.

At 1200, Front D reported:

> - Brigade 12 and Battalion 82 will start advance in direction of Abu Ageila at 14:00.
> - Brigade 1 will attack Hill 84 tonight.
> - Request for air support – bomb El Arish and Gaza at 2000... absolute air cover against enemy aircraft during tomorrow; bomb Khan Yunes, Dir Balah, El Arish and Rafah [during tomorrow].

RAID FALUJA

1211–1354	69	1601	Raisin Ben Porat Harris Cuburnek attack Faluja with 38*A50 bombs Lichtman Goldstein Aronson

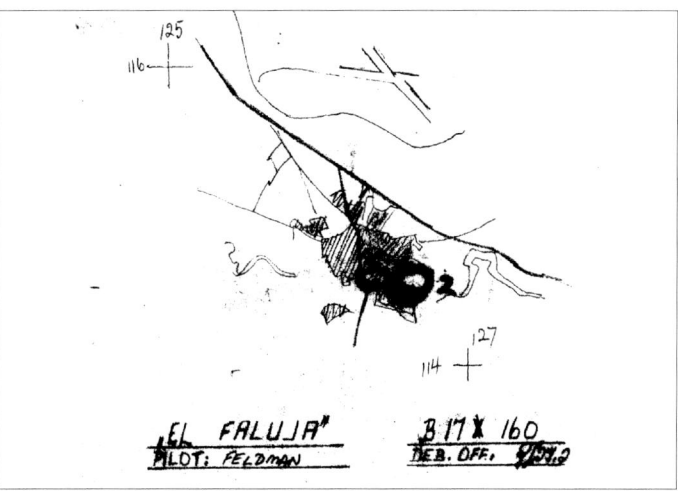

Squadron 69 Sam Feldman's crew added this scheme to their debrief report showing hits during the first bombing run over Faluja town at noon on 28 December 1948 (the smaller circle numbered '1' at the south section of town) and second run hits (the larger circle numbered '2' over the south-east section of town). Faluja airfield has been loosely sketched across the road to the north of town.

Faluja under attack - when this photo was taken is not yet known – with the former RAF station clearly visible north of the town; the direction of the shadows indicates that this photo was taken during noon to afternoon hours.

				Meyerson
				Duboff Gershaw Kaplan
1212–1347	69	1603		Noach Maseng Bresslof Weissbrod
				attack Faluja with 34*A50 bombs
				Kahn Spicehandler Ber Swiel Jacobson
1214–1345	69	1602		Feldman Ratushniak Jacobs Michel
				attack Faluja with 34*AP bombs
				Fink Lowenberg Soltan Nash
				Jackson Lazarus
1215–1230	1	0702	Solarsh Zavadi	training
1235–1355	101	2302/41	Goodlin	escort Squadron 69
1245–1355	101	2008/15	Feldman	ditto

Squadron 69's B-17s did not fly a bombing mission for 40 hours, from 1525 on 26 December until 1211 on 28 December.

The B-17 crews reported weather as cloudy and fair; visibility was reported as fair, good and poor. The B-17s bombed from 10,000 feet and each bomber flew two runs between 1255 and 1311. The leader dropped six bombs during the first run; two more bombs were:

> lying loose in bomb bay [and] were jettisoned off Nebi Yunes into the sea.

Noach's crew dropped four bombs during the first run and Feldman's added 10 bombs. There was no opposition; with no enemy aircraft and no AAA fire. All remaining bombs were dropped during the second run. The Squadron 101 pilots monitored the bombing, as ILAFI reported:

> Visibility was good. Escorted bombers over target and observed hits from south-west corner to south-east corner of Faluja town.

OBSERVATION JUDEA

| 1237–1500 | 3 | 0405 | Moller | observation |

Squadron 3 0405 was tasked to monitor activity at Judea – which was mostly in Jordanian hands but where Egyptian forces were also present, so an attempt to breakthrough from the Faluja Pocket in the direction of Judea, or an offensive from Judea with an objective to link-up with the Faluja Pocket, were options that the ILDF had to consider. As ILAFI reported:

> Radio contact was maintained with [ILDF] Beit Jibrin police station. No fortifications or people were seen in Tarqumiya. Something resembling a road block was observed at the Bet Lehem, Hebron, Beit Jibrin crossroads. Twelve stone road blocks were observed on Idna/Dawayma road, outside Idna. About three kilometers south-east of Beit Jibrin, two loaded camels and four Arabs in civilian dress were seen traveling towards Beith Jibrin. On Idna Dura road near Idna, about six to eight Arabs were seen walking towards Idna. About two kilometers north-west of Idna, 20 to 30 Bedouin tents were seen. People were walking among them. One-and-a-half kilometers south-east of Tarqumiya, 15 to 20 Bedouin tents were observed; and two to three kilometers east of Idna; two groups of 15 to 20 tents each were observed on both sides of the road. In Dura, people were observed walking around. On Hebron/Dahariya road, vehicles were observed traveling in both directions. In the police station (on which there is a green flag) in Dahariya, two to three trucks were observed. At the southern entrance to Dahariya, on the western side of the road, a public building is situated in the middle of a large courtyard. Near the building two big trucks, an armored car and two to three barracks were observed. There were many vehicle tracks leading from the road. Three kilometers south-east of Beit Jibrin, an Arab squad in civilian clothing was seen walking in military formation in the direction of Idna (in the wadi). When our aircraft circled over them they scattered along the wadi. The camels seen earlier were seen going in the opposite direction. North of Beit Jibrin, bomb hits and shell hits were observed. From Beit Jibrin to Iraq Manshiya, eight vehicles of various types were observed traveling in the direction of Iraq Manshiya.

INTO EGYPT

| 1345–1630 | 2 | | Piper | Cohen | observation |
| 1400–1500 | 1 | 0702 | Solarsh Steinman | training |

Front D planned that Brigade 12 would initiate the advance from Auja to Abu Ageila at 1400, but a subsequent Front D report indicated that the actual movement started at 1330; Brigade 12 forces, advancing from Auja to Abu Ageila, soon crossed the border, penetrating Egyptian territory in Sinai; the border was reportedly crossed at 1415.

RAID FALUJA

1415–1456	3	0407		observation Faluja
1425–1454	35	1106	Gibson	
			attack Faluja with 8*50kg bombs	
1425–1454	35	1102	Soltau	ditto
1425–1454	35	1104	Kaplansky	ditto
1425–1454	35	1105	Flint	ditto
1425–1454	35	1107	Black	ditto

Squadron 3 0407 monitored the Flight 35 raid, from 1440 until 1441, as ILAFI reported:

> *Visibility was fair to good. Bombs were observed to hit area of trenches in built-up area south of Faluja airfield and on the height to the north-west of Iraq Manshiya. Leaflets were dropped after bombing, One ack ack – 20mm, inaccurate – was encountered.*

PRANGED PIPER

1430–1630	2	0404	Zibel Zamir	observation Auja Abu Ageila
1450–1520	101	0419		Hatzor Tel Nof Hatzor
1455–1735	1	1301	Ospovat	Dov Field Beer Sheba Dov Field
1500–1700	2	0408	Biran	observation Auja Abu Ageila
1515–1820	1	1306	Lahat	Dov Field Beer Sheba Dov Field
1520–1640	101	2008/15	Cohen	patrol north-east Sinai
1520–1645	101	2004/14	Doyle	ditto

The ILAF History stated that Squadron 101 pilots Cohen and Doyle attacked Brigade 12, along the way from Auja to Abu Ageila, at 1430; the first 'friendly fire' incident between ILAF and ILDF during HOREV. However, Cohen and Doyle were not in the air at 1430;

A close-up view during the bombing of Faluja, with the town to the south and the airfield to the north, during afternoon hours of a yet unknown date.

The wreckage of Squadron 2 Piper 0404 as photographed at Beer Sheba after it was transported to Beer Sheba from Auja; Squadron 2 pilot Zvi Zibel was the only ILAF fatality during HOREV.

actually, not a single Squadron 101 fighter was flying anywhere at that time. The 'friendly fire' incident probably did happen, but only later, sometime after the Squadron 101 pair departed Hatzor at 1520, as ILAFI reported:

> Visibility was hazy. Strafed a three-tonner [truck] near Bir Burg. At reported airfield south of El Arish, observed three Spitfires in pens. Made a pass at deck level at one [Spitfire] in pen. Observed a lot of tar barrels at one end of the runway and also men working on the field. Observed scattered traffic on main road traveling north to El Arish and strafed three different vehicles. Observed strikes on all three of them. Observed a large movement of transport and armored cars towards Abu Ageila. On the road from Auja... strafed transport which opened fire on the planes. These vehicles were marked with Egyptian markings. Also observed vehicles traveling south on El Arish/Auja road, north of Abu Ageila.

The convoy of vehicles that the Spitfires strafed along the road from Auja to Abu Ageila was, possibly, the Brigade 12 column that, reportedly, included former Egyptian vehicles.

Circa 1630, the two Squadron 2 Pipers tasked to support Brigade 12 encountered unidentified fighters, as ILAFI Condensed Operational Summary Number 5 reported:

> Four enemy Spits have been active in the Auja [to] Bir Asluj area. They gave chase to two Piper Cubs on a recce, following them to the landing strip at Auja. One Piper landed safely and the other pranged and nose-dived. The Spits then strafed our troops and armor in the area.

Piper 0408 was the one that landed safely. Piper 0404 was the one that crashed; Squadron 2 pilot Zvi Zibel and Brigade 12 observer Isaac Zamir were killed.

OBSERVATION FALUJA

Time	Sqn	A/C	Pilot	Mission
1550–1600	101	2018/17	Levett	Tel Nof Hatzor delivery to Squadron 101
1555–1640	1	0702	Solarsh	Dov Field Hatzor Dov Field
1600–2228	3	0405	Front (Biram)	Tel Nof Dov Field Tel Nof
1605–1625	1	0701	Efrat Porat	test
1615–1654	3	0106	Biram	training
1617–1705	3	0407	Roth	Tel Nof Hatzor observation Hatzor Tel Nof

The third VELVETTA 2 Spitfire delivered to Squadron 101 was 2018, so that by the end of 28 December the ILAF fighter squadron inventory included seven Spitfires and two P-51s, plus the five S199s that flew only five sorties from 22 to 26 December and were practically grounded at Hatzor. Squadron 3 Piper 0407 flew observation over Faluja, as ILAFI reported:

> Visibility was medium. No movement was seen on the roads east of Beit Jibrin... No movement was seen on Faluja/Iraq Manshiya road.

The Faluja Pocket and surrounding sector seemed quiet and there were no signs of an Egyptian exploitation of success, in the wake of the Operation ELIMINATION defeat, for at attempted breakthrough. Nevertheless, ILAF bombings of the Faluja Pocket continued.

RAID FALUJA

Time	Sqn	A/C	Crew / Mission
1632–1743	69	1603	Noach Feldman Bresslof Weissbrod attack Faluja with 37*A50 bombs Ber Spicehandler Kahn Swiel Jacobson
1634–1750	69	1602	McConville Spink Seftel Weinstein attack Faluja with 38*A50 bombs Cohen Christiensen Schwartzbach Robinson Liponetzky Kaplan Cohen Joffe

Squadron 69 crews reported poor weather, poor visibility over the target and a clouds base over the target of 4,500 feet, so the B-17s bombed from 4,500 feet and 4,000 feet, much lower than usual.

The first bomber was over the target from 1703 until 1704, the second from 1715 to 1716. AAA over the target was reported as light, scattered and inaccurate.

The crew of 1603 flew one bombing run, heading 115, and reported four hang-ups and nine duds, but it was too dark for a second run over the target so the four hang-ups were jettisoned over the sea on the way back to Ramat David. The debrief report of 1603 concluded with a complaint:

Crew complains very bad blackout at Kfar Joshua [west of Ramat David]. Correction: NO BLACKOUT.

The second crew also flew a single run, heading 115, as indicated in the debrief report:

Bombs overshot slightly due to some failure in electrical release circuit. 18 bombs fell safe due to f... poor arming wires. This is a standard complaint!!! Cannot something be done?????

END OF DAY 6

1712–1846	103	1405	Orringer Keidar Adler Lipman attack Faluja with 16*100 [AQ59a: 100lb or kg?]bombs	
1715–2225	1	1301	Machnes	Dov Field Beer Sheba Dov Field
1730–00:01	106	RX-138	Moonitz	VELVETTA 2 Niksic Tel Nof
1815–1945	103	1401	Shatkai Wygle Segal Aronson attack Faluja with 16*100 [AQ60a: 100lb or kg?]bombs	
1930–0815	1	1306	Ospovat	Dov Field Beer Sheba Dov Field

Squadron 103 1405 reported cloudy weather and good visibility over its target; the C-47 was over Faluja from 1803 until 1836 and bombed from 2,500 feet, as indicated in debrief:

B-17 1602 flew two missions to Faluja on 28 December 1948. Sam Feldman piloted 1602 on both missions, in the first with co-pilot Jack Ratushniak and in the second as co-pilot to Issy Noach.

First run [heading] 150. Eight bombs dropped across northern sector of town just south of road, all bombs observed hitting town.
Due to conditions of darkness, could not relocate Faluja after first drop. Returned to Tel Nof and made another run over target.
Second run [heading] 170. Eight bombs dropped opposite center of town.

Squadron 103 1401 reported bad visibility over the target, was over Faluja from 1920 until 1927 and bombed from 2,500 feet, as indicated in debrief:

First run [heading] 120. Eight bombs dropped across target.
Second run [heading] 100. Eight bombs dropped across target.
Pilot request flares to be dropped on dark nights.

Both Squadron 103 C-47 crews reported absence of AAA fire.

Day 6 ended with mixed feelings. HOREV forces completed occupation of the Auja sector and penetrated Sinai, but ELIMINATION's failure thwarted ambitions to launch an offensive at Front B and forced the ILAF to focus on suppression of the Faluja Pocket. From 0750 until 1920, the ILAF launched 30 sorties – 23 T-6 sorties, five B-17 sorties and two C-47 sorties – to bomb Faluja; an effort that may have been more effective if launched in preparation for ELIMINATION, or if aimed to pin down Egyptian forces during ELIMINATION, than in the aftermath of ELIMINATION's bloody failure.

For the first time during HOREV, EGAF fighters were sighted during daylight, over battlefields, on two occasions: during the morning with a probable objective to support the Faluja Pocket during ELIMINATION, and during the afternoon over HOREV forces in the Auja sector. By then the EGAF retreated from El Arish, the recently reported El Riah airfield was most likely nothing more than a decoy and EGAF fighters operated from Bir Hama, though this redeployment was not yet known to the ILAF during Day 6.

The morning appearance of the EGAF ended in air combat and the ILAF credited three kills, though a more realistic result was one kill.

The afternoon appearance of EGAF fighters over Faluja resulted in the loss of Squadron 2's 0404; the first ILAF combat loss during HOREV.

Two new C-47s boosted the ILAF ORBAT on 28 December.

Four Squadron 106 C-46s flew nine round trips – Tel Nof Niksic Tel Nof - during VELVETTA 2; these two C-46s were photographed at Niksic, the nearest is probably RX-138/1708.

Richard Kohnke flew C-47 NC61190 from Athens, via Nicosia, to Haifa. Harold Auerbach landed C-47 NC63186 at Tel Nof, at 1755, at the end of a flight from Ajaccio.

DAY 7
29 DECEMBER 1948

HOREV's objective for Day 7 was Abu Ageila, an important crossroads some 20 kilometers deep into Sinai, from where roads ranged to El Arish in the north-west and Bir Hama in the south-west.

RAID FALUJA

0325–1000	106	RX-137	Keren	VELVETTA 2 Tel Nof Niksic
0344–1015	106	RX-130	Ford	VELVETTA 2 Tel Nof Niksic
0527–0625	103	1405	Orringer Keidar Adler Lipman attack Faluja with 16*100kg bombs	
0557–0647	103	1401	Shatkai Wygle Segal Aronson attack Faluja with 16*100kg bombs	
0559–0703	3	0409	Dankner	observation Faluja

Squadron 103 C-47s, tasked to raid Faluja, took off from nearby Tel Nof and were over Faluja from 0537 until 0538 and 0601 until 0606; sunrise was at 06:37, so C-47 crews benefited from ILDF searchlights that marked the target.

The 1405 crew reported good weather, good visibility, no AAA fire and bombing from 3,000 feet, as indicated in its debrief:

> Searchlights from Julis and Hulikat converging on south side of airfield were of assistance. Sufficient light at time of bombing for adequate vision. Bombs fell across target...

The 1401 crew also reported good weather, good visibility, no AAA fire and bombing from 3,000 feet, as revealed in its debrief:

> First run [heading] 120... stick hit south of main road... four doubles dropped...
> Second run [heading] 130. Dropped approximately 150 to 200 meters south of road across town... eight bombs dropped. Usual explosions seen. No fires seen.

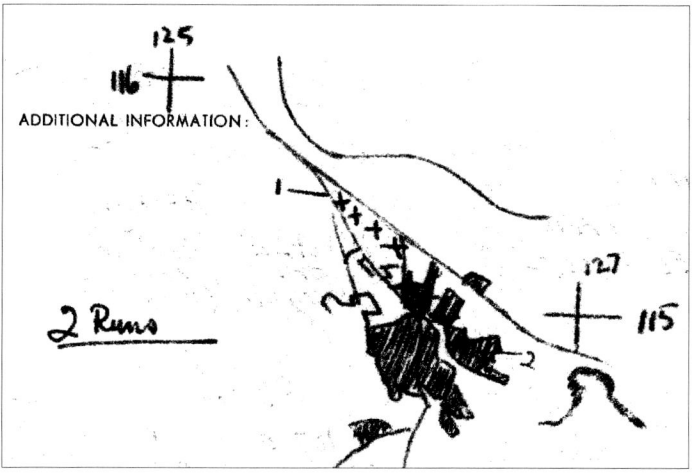

The Squadron 103 C-47 1401 crew added this sketch to debrief of the 29 December 1948 mission to bomb Faluja, illustrating two bombing runs over Faluja town from 0601 until 0606.

Upon completion of their mission, the two C-47s returned home to Ramat David.

The Squadron 3 Piper was tasked to monitor activity in the Faluja Pocket, as ILAFI reported:

> No movement of vehicles or people was observed in Faluja or Iraq Manshiya; 20mm ack ack was encountered from a north-west direction.

ABU AGEILA IN OUR HANDS

0600–0745	2	Piper	Rubens	observation Auja Abu Ageila
0700–1541	3	0110	Moller	Tel Nof Dov Field Tel Nof
07:27–0810	3	0409	Simantov	training

Brigade 12 entered Abu Ageila, reportedly at 0600 though occupation of Abu Ageila may have been completed a little later, since Squadron 2 Piper was tasked to support the brigade with monitoring enemy forces in that sector, past the reported occupation time, as ILAFI reported:

> Visibility over target [Abu Ageila] was good. Purpose of recce was to observe enemy in Abu Ageila. A concentration of vehicles was observed north-west of tent camp in Abu Ageila... In the village, seven scattered vehicles were observed and very few people were noticed walking about the village. Long convoys belonging to us were observed along Auja/Abu Ageila road. Details were reported to Brigade 12 Intelligence Officer during flight. At 0710 Spitfires appeared and our aircraft flew away.

The observed Spitfires were most likely Egyptian, since Squadron 101 Spitfire take-offs did not start until 0750.

RAID RAFAH

0730–0935	69	1601	Raisin Ben Porat Harris Cuburnek attack Rafah with 2*250kg+22*50kg bombs Lichtman Goldstein Aronson Meyerson Duboff Gershaw
0730–0935	69	1602	Feldman Ratushniak Jacobs Michel attack Rafah with 2*250kg+28*A50 bombs Soltan Lowenberg Fink Lazarus Nash Jackson
0743–0945	69	1603	McConville Spink Seftel Weinstein attack Rafah with 2*A250+22*A50 bombs Cohen Christiensen Schwartzbach Cohen Robinson Kaplan Liponetzky Kapusa
0745–0925	101	2302/41	Dangott escort Squadron 69
0750–0925	101	2008/15	Goodlin ditto

1601 crew was over Rafah from 0846 until 0849; the weather was cloudy and visibility was described as good through breaks in the clouds. The B-17 bombed Rafah camp from 15,500 feet in face of AAA that was reported as very accurate.

1602 flew a dummy bomb run over Khan Yunes from 0838 until

Squadron 69 gunner Wilfred Jackson flew 25 missions; many of these with fellow gunners Joe Lazarus and Stanley Nash. Jackson was wounded over Rafah on 29 December 1948 when an Egyptian AAA damaged B-17 1602. This view captures Wilfred Jackson (sitting on the stairway), Joe Lazarus (in white shirt) and navigator Tim Michel (with binoculars) at the Hammers' austere living quarters.

0839 and was over the target from 0848 to 0849; the crew reported that the weather was bad, visibility was poor and the bombing run was flown at 15,500 feet, but only half the bombs onboard 1602 were dropped as there was hang-up for a whole side of the bomb bay. The half that dropped overshot Rafah. AAA was described as:

> Heavy, very accurate; 88[mm]; ship hit... one [waist] gunner [Wilfred Jackson] wounded.

1603 reported fair visibility and fair weather, and bombed from 15,500 feet from 0848 until 0849 in the face of accurate AAA that inflicted minor damage – a small hole in the tail – while four of the bombs fell safe. The Squadron 101 pilots reported the sighting of two unidentified aircraft, as indicated in the debrief report:

> Proceeded to rendezvous, observed what appeared to be a twin-engined aircraft eight to 10 [miles] out to sea south of Tel Aviv. Fighters tried to chase him but he was lost in clouds. Then escorted B-17s – who were 15 minutes late for rendezvous – to target but did not observe their bombing results. During the bombers' second run, observed an unidentified fighter approaching from west. As fighter approached formation, the Mustang tried to chase him but the fighter was too far away and too fast, and the Mustang returned to formation. Escorted the bombers back to rendezvous point and then returned to base.

RAID FALUJA

0747–0825	35	1106	Gibson	attack Faluja with 8*50kg bombs
0747–0818	35	1102	Soltau	ditto
0747–0825	35	1104	Dougherty	ditto
0747–0818	35	1105	Flint	ditto
0747–0818	35	1107	Black	ditto

Flight 35 T-6 1104 was damaged in a landing accident at 0825 on 29 December 1948 upon return to Tel Nof from a mission over Faluja.

T-6 at Tel Nof; the ILAFI post-HOREV summary stated that Flight 35 T-6s flew 96 attack sorties out of 243 attack sorties that the ILAF flew during HOREV.

0750–0910	1	0603)	Renov	Dov Field Ramat David Dov Field
0752–0830	3	0407	Dankner	observation Faluja
0800–0855	101	2004/14	Weizman	escort Flight 35
0800–0855	101	2002/11	Levett	ditto

The ILDF intercepted messages from the Faluja Pocket indicating no intention to attempt a breakthrough, yet the ILAF continued to bomb the pocket. Flight 35 attacked from 0750 to 0751, as ILAFI reported:

> Visibility was good. Two runs were made over target. On first run, aircraft released four bombs each and bombs exploded around target. On second run, aircraft released remaining four bombs, each [of] which exploded very near to target.

Upon return to Tel Nof, 1104 was damaged in a landing accident; Oded Abarbanell – at the time a Flight 35 pilot – recalled in his memoirs:

> The Harvard was a very robust aircraft and our only loss resulted from explosion of our own bomb. Richard Dougherty... returned to Tel Nof from a mission with one bomb hang up... Dougherty... turned west and tried to jettison the bomb over the sea, but to no avail. There being no other choice, Dougherty returned to land. When he was at an altitude of approximately two meters above runway, and just before the aircraft wheels touched the surface of the runway, the bomb dropped and exploded. Dougherty was probably prepared for such an occurrence as he immediately opened up the throttle for maximum engine power, pushed down the rudder pedal with his right leg and retracted undercarriage while sliding

the aircraft to the right, towards the mud field to the right of the runway where he performed a perfect belly landing... we all ran to the aircraft and were sure that Dougherty was at least injured, but miraculously he exited the cockpit without a scratch, even though the aircraft was full of holes.

1104 was not repaired and never flew again. Squadron 3 0407 was tasked to monitor the Flight 35 raid, as ILAFI reported:

> Visibility was good. The object of the operation was a recce of the results of the bombing by AT-6s of the school in Iraq Manshiya. Each aircraft was observed to dive twice on target. Most of the hits were very close to the buildings. After bombing, the smoke dispersed and one building, somewhat destroyed, was seen. The big building was seen damaged. An explosion was seen in the vicinity, not from the bombing.

Squadron 101 pilots Weizman and Levett were to escort the Flight 35 raid, as ILAFI reported:

> Visibility was poor. Observed Harvards drop their bombs between Faluja and Iraq Manshiya, apparently on entrenched positions. After escorting aircraft back to base, proceeded to Auja and patrolled the Auja and Nirim areas.

Interestingly, the Squadron 3 Piper take-off time was reported as 0752 and the Squadron 101 take-off time was reported as 0800, while the Flight 35 reported TOT was 0750 to 0751! Either watches were not synchronized or reports were inaccurate.

RAID FALUJA

0930–1325	1	1306	Kaplan	Dov Field Tel Nof Beer Sheba Dov Field
0935–1324	3	0409	Katzin	Tel Nof Ramat David Tel Nof
1010–1120	1	0702	Efrat Lavi	training
1015–1335	1	1301	Solarsh	Dov Field Beer Sheba Dov Field
1030–1052	35	1106	Gibson	attack Faluja with 8*50kg bombs
1030–1052	35	1102	Soltau	ditto
1030–1052	35	1105	Flint	ditto
1030–1052	35	1107	Black	ditto

Flight 35 returned to Faluja, with four T-6s, from 1040 to 1041. ILAFI reported:

> Visibility was fair. One run was made by each aircraft over target. Thirty-one bombs were dropped over target area, four of which were observed to hit 20mm ack ack positions and four to hit positions of the 25-lb guns, and the remainder around target. An explosion was observed after hitting ack ack gun. One bomb, owing to hang-up, was later dropped over the airfield.

EL ARISH AND EL RIAH

1040–1130	1	1304	Renov	Dov Field Beer Sheba
1046–1145	3	0407	Front	training
1050–1220	101	2008	Peake	patrol north-east Sinai
1055–1220	101	2004	Augarten	patrol north-east Sinai

Squadron 1's Rapide 1304 was damaged in a landing accident at Beer Sheba. Squadron 101 pilots Augarten and Peake patrolled north-east Sinai, as ILAFI reported:

> Visibility was good. At Auja, observed scattered transport, also on the road to Abu Ageila. Observed large concentrations of our vehicles north-west of Abu Ageila about three kilometers on road to El Arish. Scattered vehicles seen moving on road towards El Arish. At El Arish, observed six aircraft in pen and one fighter on field and one Dakota in pen. The small [El Riah] field [south of El Arish] was in the same condition as it was on 28 December. Observed same three Spitfires at El Arish. Three fighters in pens on either end of the short runway. Heavy flak was encountered at Dir Balah.

The ILAFI report seems to have been a little confused due to a disrupted copy of the Squadron 101 debrief report; the more likely observations were the same three Spitfires at El Riah to the south of El Arish and six Spitfires in pens at El Arish, plus a fighter on the field

Squadron 101, Hatzor, winter of 1948 to 1949. Back row from left to right: Lee Sinclair, Slick Goodlin, Syd Cohen and Technical Officer Harry Axelrod. Front row from left to right: William Schroeder, Jack Doyle, Waine Peake and Arnold Ruch; Peake flew seven missions during HOREV, the first of these was with Rudy Augarten on 29 December 1948.

Aaron Remez, a Second World War RAF fighter pilot, was ILAF Commander from 1948 until 1950.

and a C-47 in a pen, also at El Arish, as indicated in the Squadron 101 debrief report:

> Flew straight to Auja. Scattered transport there. Scattered transport on road to Abu Ageila. Three vehicles about three miles west of Abu Ageila. Saw large concentration of our vehicles (18 stationary vehicles) north-west of Abu Ageila about three kilometers on road towards El Arish. Vehicle burning just off road on way to El Arish... Scattered vehicles, six to seven, on road six miles towards El Arish. One vehicle moving on road towards El Arish. At El Arish observed six aircraft (fighters) in pens and one fighter on field and one Dakota in pen. Small [El Riah] field in same condition as yesterday. Same three Spits. At El Arish, three fighters in pens on either end of short runway. Heavy flak at Dir Balah.

OBSERVATION JUDEA

1147–1354 3 0405 Giladi observation

Piper 0405 was tasked to monitor activity at Judea, an area that inspired some of the longest and more detailed debriefs, as ILAFI reported:

> Visibility was fair to bad. At Tarqumiya, a stone road block was observed... A truck encircling the road block from the south was observed. At... a wooded hill was observed. At the bottom of the hill, two tents and three vehicles were observed and in the wood about six tents and three trucks were also observed. On the hill close to the wadi there is a white tent. At Idna... four trucks were observed in the village and a great number of people and nine stone road blocks. Between Idna and Tarqumiya, two Bedouin camps each containing 15 tents were observed. At Dahariya, near the police station north-east of the village, two vehicles and two tents were observed. South-east of the village are tents and vehicles and possible troop movements. West of the road there is a building with a tin roof, two vehicles and trenches. On Dura/Hebron road a great number of people were observed walking in both directions, and in the village a group of buildings were observed (school?) near the wood. Four tents and vehicles were observed in the yard. There was movement of people there. At Beit Jibrin, a large movement of our vehicles was noted and a low wing aircraft was observed flying towards Faluja.

SCRAMBLE TO ABU AGEILA

1150–1325	101	2302/41	Senior	scramble to Abu Ageila
1150–1155	101	2001/10		scramble to Abu Ageila, aborted, RTB
1150–1325	101	2002/11	Feldman	scramble to Abu Ageila
1155–1335	101	2301/40		scramble to Abu Ageila

The EGAF was reportedly particularly active over Abu Ageila on 29 December; some time during that day, Brigade 12 reported:

> Our forces were bombed by a four-engined aircraft, escorted by two fighters, and one soldier was injured.

Squadron 101, Hatzor, winter. Front row from left to right: Jack Cohen and Seymour Feldman; Feldman flew 15 missions during HOREV.

If this sighting was correct, then this is the only thus far reported daytime mission of an EGAF four-engined bomber, most likely a Stirling. Of the four fighters that Squadron 101 scrambled circa 1150, Boris Senior and Seymour Feldman teamed together, as indicated in debrief:

> In formation straight to Abu Ageila. Dived under cloud from sun. No enemy aircraft to be seen. No transport on road from Abu Ageila to [Suez] Canal. Two convoys moving towards El Arish from Abu Ageila. Distance five to 10 kilometers between the two convoys. Number of Jeeps in convoy nearest Abu Ageila. Other convoy had an ambulance with red crescent marking in middle of convoy, were about 30 vehicles in this convoy. About 20 to 30 [vehicles] in convoy nearest Abu Ageila. Armor in both convoys but more in convoy nearest El Arish... Three vehicles at head nearest El Arish were nearly burnt out. Feldman jumped by FIAT, no strikes. FIAT ran away. Field south of El Arish still same three aircraft and no signs of activity of any sort. Pipeline at... burst near sulphur quarries, water gushing from it. When leader went down to investigate... Feldman stayed up to cover and was jumped by a FIAT, which made one pass and disappeared south. Saw two Pipers at Auja field, one completely burnt-out and other seemed unharmed.

The burnt-out Piper at Auja was 0404 that crashed there the previous day. The two convoys reported along the road from Abu Ageila to El Arish may have been Israeli (the one closer to Abu Ageila) and Egyptian (the one closer to El Arish), with the former advancing from Abu Ageila and the latter retreating to El Arish.

RAIDS FROM ABU AGEILA

1200–1410	1	0702	Efrat	Dov Field Tel Nof Dov Field
1205–1235	1	1302	Steinman	test bombing
1215–1245	3	0407	Rosen	training

ISRAELI AIR FORCE IN THE 1948 WAR—ISRAELI WINTER OFFENSIVE OPERATION HOREV 22 DECEMBER 1948–7 JANUARY 1949

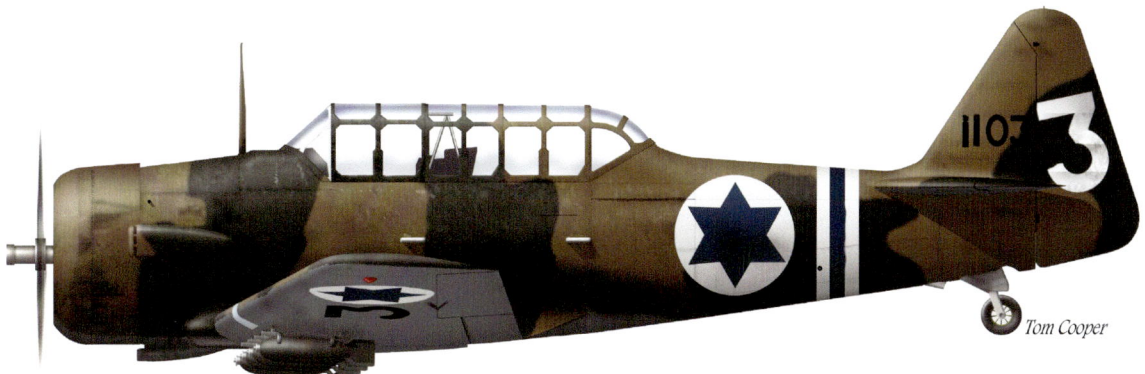

Six North American T-6A Texans were smuggled from the USA to Israel in November 1948. All were painted in dark brown (probably BS381C/450) and dark green (BS381C/641A) on upper surfaces, and medium sea grey (BS381C/641) on undersurfaces. They were fitted with eight underwing bomb racks for bombs calibre 25kg (50lbs) and a pair of machine guns calibre 7.62mm.

In November 1948, the IDF/AF introduced four-digit serials, and its Texans – used as dive-bombers – received those in range 1100. Last number was repeated on the rudder and upper surface of the left wing in white, and lower suface of the left wing in black. While originally applied on the rear fuselage only, roundels appeared on wing surfaces during November 1948, after arrival of Spitfires within frame of 'Operation Velvetta'.

Also clandestinely acquired from the USA were four B-17s, discovered on a dump in Florida. Brought up to flying condition, three were flown via the Azores to Zatek in Czechoslovakia, where they received instrumentation and make-shift armament. Because it was in worst condition, this example was given a complete, even if crude re-paint in light stone (BS381C/361), dark brown (BS381C/450) and the same green as used on Avia S.199s (RAL6013) on upper surfaces. Bottom surfaces were painted in unspecified bluish grey colour. Sometimes in November-December 1948 period it received the artwork of Mickey Mouse on the fin.

Another B-17 to receive a complete re-paint was the example serialled 1603. Because only black & white photographs are available, details of its new colours are not entirely clear, but it is believed to have been painted in light stone (BS381C/361), dark brown (BS381C/450) on upper surfaces and sides, and the same bluish grey colour on undersurfaces. As usually, full serial was applied in blue. Roundels were added on underwing surfaces by January 1949.

Colour profile commentaries and images by Tom Cooper.

MIDDLE EAST@WAR VOLUME 2

Ten Curtis C-46 Commandos were the first heavy transports to serve with the IDF/AF. They were acquired from USAF surplus stocks and smuggled to Israel with help of fake registrations of the Panamanian airline LAPSA. By late 1948, their top sides were camouflaged in olive green, while undersurfaces were left in natural metal. Some examples – like RX-134 shown here – still wore full LAPSA registrations.

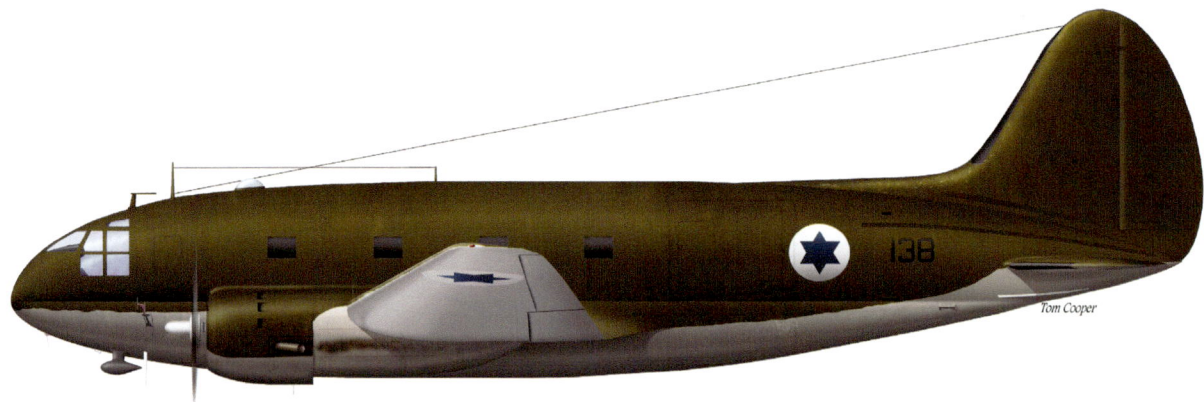

The C-46 with serial number 138 is probably one of best-known Israeli Commandos. Camouflaged olive green on top surfaces and sides (applied with brush and in quite crude fashion), it was nicknamed 'Shosh' (the name was applied on the right side of the nose, in Hebrew, directly below the windscreen). They were primarily used for hauling new equipment and supplies from Czechoslovakia to Israel.

The second North American P-51D Mustang acquitted by the Israelis originally received the serial 2302, then D-191 and finally 41, as shown here. Left in natural metal overall, with the usual 'anti-glare panel' painted in black, by the end of the war it was nick-named 'Gedy' and wore two kill markings (one for a REAF C-47 Dakota claimed in November 1948, and another for a Macchi 205 claimed in January 1949).

Also left in natural metal overall, the first Israeli P-51D (registration 2301) still wore its original serial, 'D-190' as of January 1949. Originally nicknamed 'Zulu' it was re-named 'Tink' (short for Tinkerbell of Peter Pan fame) by December, and received full markings of No. 101 Squadron on spinner and rudder. National insignia was originally worn on the fuselage only, but in November 1948 applied on wing surfaces too.

Colour profile commentaries and images by Tom Cooper.

ISRAELI AIR FORCE IN THE 1948 WAR—ISRAELI WINTER OFFENSIVE OPERATION HOREV 22 DECEMBER 1948–7 JANUARY 1949

Israel obtained 20 Piper PA-11-90 Cubs in September 1948. These were rushed into service painted in green and brown camouflage on top surfaces and sides, and light blue on undersurfaces. National insignia was applied only to the bottom of the wing and fuselage sides. Most were equipped with makeshift bomb-racks for carriage of up to 60kg bombs. This example wore the insignia of the 'Flying Camel' Squadron. Its full serial was 0520.

While retaining their greyish-green camouflage of RAL6013 Avia Green (or RLM68) the few Avia S.199s still in service in late 1948 wore significantly different markings than at earlier times. These included large serials applied on the rear fuselage, and disproportionally large roundels.

The Avia S.199 'D-121' did not follow the trend of ever larger serials, but – contrary to its looks duringthe summer of 1948 – did receive full markings of the No. 101 'First Fighter' Squadron, including spinner in red, and red and white stripes on the rudder. Notable is that the serial was applied in black and blue colours, and that the 'Red Cross' insignia over the first-aid package was replaced with the Star of David applied in red.

While based at Qastina airfield in late 1948 and early 1949, the Avia S.199 'D-123' was severely weathered and already received some patches of fresh colour, as well as disproportionally large roundels.

Colour profile commentaries and images by Tom Cooper.

This Spitfire LF.Mk.IXe arrived in Israel during the Operation Velvetta, wearing standard RAF camouflage colours – consisting of ocean grey (FS16187) and dark green (BS381C/641) over medium sea grey (BS381C/637) – and full markings of No. 101 'First Fighter' Squadron. Originally serialled 2003, it received a large identification number 12d (possibly applied in yellow, instead in white) on the rear fuselage, while at Hatzor AB, in December 1949.

Another delivery of the Operation Velvetta I was this Spitfire LF.Mk.IXe. While otherwise left in standard RAF camouflage, by January 1949 it received identification bands on the bottom of the wings. Notable is the original serial (2004) applied in black underneath horizontal stabilizer.

While generally similar in appearance and colours to all the other Spitfire LF.Mk.IXes in service with No. 101 Squadron as of early 1949, this example (serial 2011, identification number 26, delivered within the frame of 'Operation Velveta II') received personal art too, in form of an Eagle clutching a Spitfire. While not receiving the patch of the No. 101 Squadron, it had its original serial applied in white, underneath the horizontal stabilizer.

Assembled from parts abandoned by the RAF, the Spitfire Mk.IVc with serial number D-131 as seen at Herzlyia, in October 1948. The aircraft was either painted in Avia Green (RAL6013) or dark green primer, except for undersurfaces of the wing. It wore no national insignia, and small serials, applied with brush, on the rear fuselage. Technicians chalked the name 'Israel' and various other inscriptions around the aircraft.

Colour profile commentaries and images by Tom Cooper.

ISRAELI AIR FORCE IN THE 1948 WAR—ISRAELI WINTER OFFENSIVE OPERATION HOREV 22 DECEMBER 1948–7 JANUARY 1949

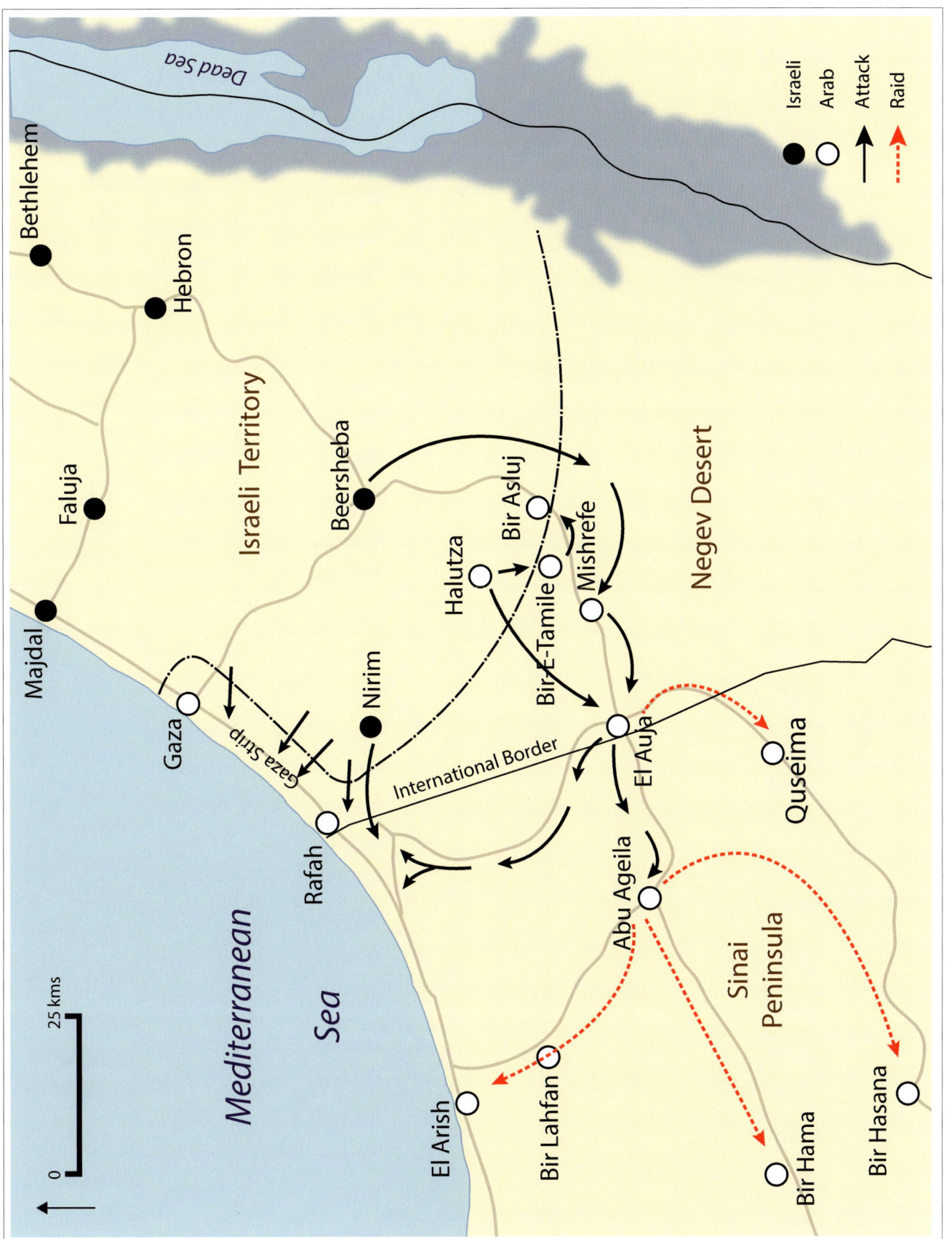

A map of Operation HOREV Phase 2 - during which the ILDF advanced from Auja to Abu Ageila and raided El Riah nearby Bir Lahfan, Bir Hama, Bir Hasana and Quseima; by the end of this phase an American/British ultimatum forced Israel to order the ILDF to retreat from Abu Ageila to Auja and, as an alternative, to launch an attack from Auja to Rafah in order to cut the EGDF in the Gaza Strip or, even better, to force the EGDF to retreat from the Gaza Strip.

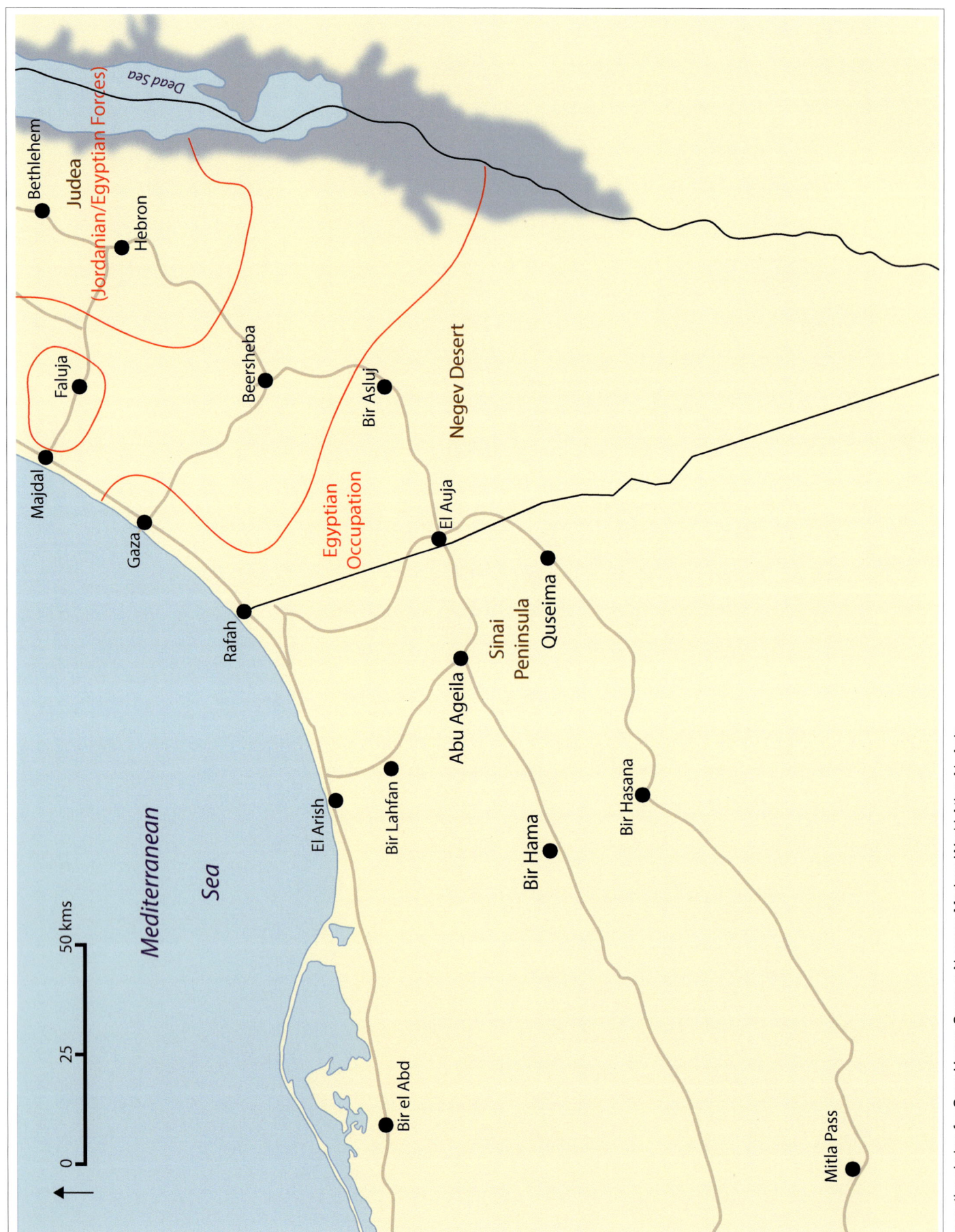

Operational plan for Opor Horev. Source: Newnes Modern World Atlas Al_Auja

ISRAELI AIR FORCE IN THE 1948 WAR—ISRAELI WINTER OFFENSIVE OPERATION HOREV 22 DECEMBER 1948–7 JANUARY 1949

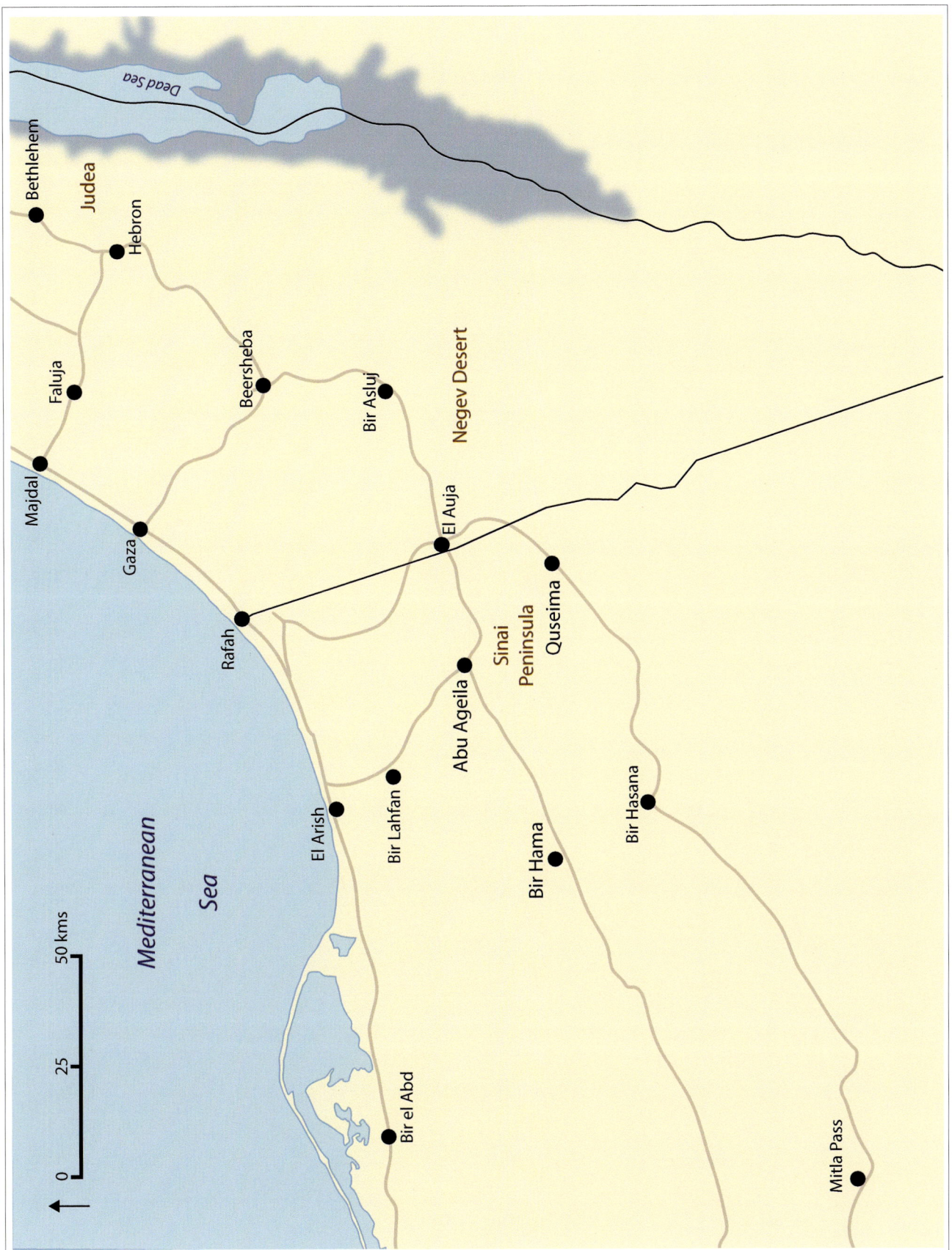

The final phase of HOREV was an ILDF pincer attack in the direction of Rafah aimed to force the EGDF to retreat from the Gaza Strip or, if the EGDF would not retreat, to turn the Gaza Strip into another Faluja Pocket. Brigade 12 attacked from Auja in the direction of Rafah Junction west of Rafah and Brigade 1 attacked from the Imara sector in the direction east of Rafah. Source: Newnes Modern World Atlas Al_Auja

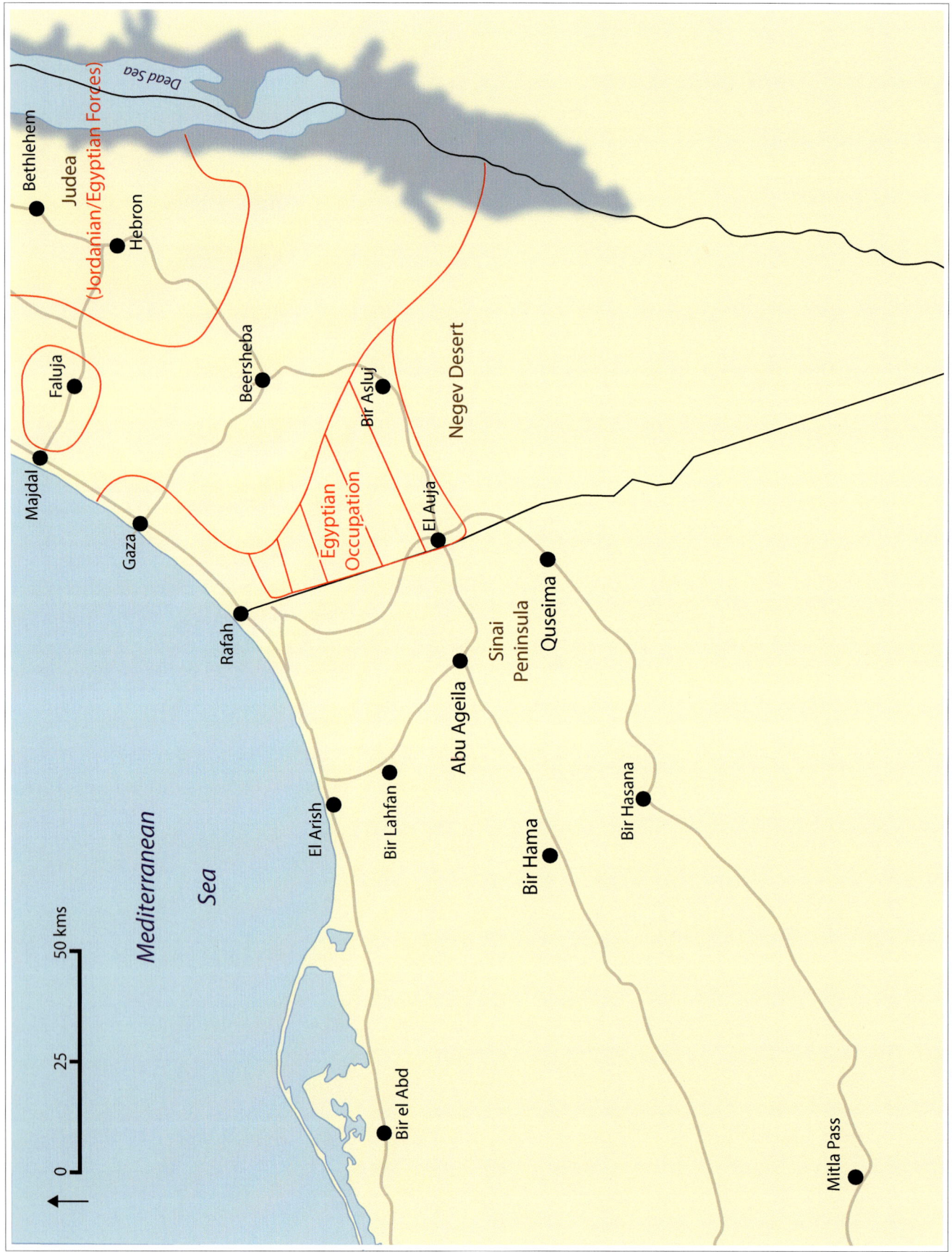

Israel gained ground during HOREV, but failed to eliminate the Faluja Pocket and to dislodge the EGDF from the Gaza Strip, yet the ILDF HOREV offensive forced Egypt to abandon hardline policy: to seek a ceasefire; and to agree to negotiate with Israel. Practically, ILDF HOREV ended the 1948 Palestine War/Israel War for Independence. Source: Newnes Modern World Atlas Al_Auja

Front D forces at Abu Ageila actually launched two raids circa 1230; both tasked to assault EGAF air bases in north-east Sinai.

A Brigade 8 Battalion 82 task force was tasked to advance north-west, from Abu Ageila to El Riah airfield (nearby Bir Lahfan some 30 kilometers from Abu Ageila) in the direction of El Arish (some 45 kilometers from Abu Ageila). A Brigade 12 Battalion 7 task force was to raid Bir Hama airfield; this airfield was not yet known to the ILAF and its existence was exposed during initial interrogation, at Abu Ageila, of an Egyptian prisoner of war who stated that the airfield was new, hosted five aircraft, was some 60 kilometers south-west of Abu Ageila, along the road from Abu Ageila to Ismailia, to the north of the road, and was not well defended. Based on this information, the Battalion 7 task force was ordered to occupy the airfield overnight so that, the next morning, an ILAF aircraft with pilots would land at Bir Hama, the pilots would fly away the captured aircraft, the Battalion 7 task force would destroy the airfield and then retreat to Abu Ageila.

RAID FALUJA

1240–1319	35	1106	Gibson	attack Faluja with 8*50kg bombs
1240–1319	35	1102	Soltau	ditto
1240–1319	35	1105	Flint	ditto
1240–1319	35	1107	Black	ditto

Flight 35's harassment of Faluja continued from 1305 to 1306, as ILAFI reported:

> Visibility was fair to good. Aircraft made one run each and released eight bombs each. South-west portion of target was hit. Scattered hits were also observed beyond target area. All bombs exploded.

EL RIAH IN OUR HANDS

1255–1310	1	1302	Steinman	test bombing
1255–1315	3	0114	Ruff Rotem	training
1357–1610	3	0407	Biram	Tel Nof Dov Field Tel Nof
1450–1605	101	0419		Hatzor Dov Field Hatzor
1509–1707	3	0405	Navot	observation Faluja

The Battalion 82 task force reported, at 1315, the 'discovery' of an enemy airfield; this was actually El Riah airfield, near Bir Lahfan, south of El Arish, where ILAF pilots reported, on a number of occasions, three seemingly-static fighters in pens. This task force then attacked El Riah airfield. At 1430, Front D reported:

> Brigade 12: arrived at airfield 20 kilometers from Abu Ageila in direction of El Arish. Found four enemy aircraft. Send pilots and engineers to collect them.

By 1500 the airfield was in the hands of the Battalion 82 task force. The four captured enemy aircraft turned out to be one unserviceable Spitfire, EGAF Number 664, and three Spitfire dummies. Supply and ordnance – bombs and rounds – were also captured but, at the time, El Riah was almost certainly not an operational air base and was probably used as a decoy aimed to divert ILAF attention from El Arish – which by then was probably no longer operational – and Bir Hama, which replaced El Arish as the EGAF's main base in north-east Sinai. A fine illustration of the problematic nature of military

ILDF troops examine EGAF Number 664, a Spitfire in a pen, captured on 29 December 1948 when El Riah was occupied.

Spitfire EGAF Number 664 was unserviceable when captured by the ILDF at El Riah on 29 December 1948; it was the only real aircraft at El Riah.

reports as they surface up the command chain, ILPM David Ben-Gurion wrote in his diary:

> A telegram from the front informs that five Egyptian aircraft were found in a deserted airfield, pilots are requested to come and collect them.

RAID EL ARISH

1510–1735	69	1601	Raisin Ben Porat Harris Cuburnek	attack El Arish with 30*100lb bombs
			Lichtman Goldstein Aronson	
			Meyerson Duboff Gershaw Cohen	
1510–1735	69	1602	Feldman Ratushniak Jacobs Michel	attack El Arish with 26*100lb bombs
			Soltan Lowenberg Fink Lazarus	
			Nash Meyerson Joffe	
1515–1710	1	0412	Lahat	Dov Field Beer Sheba Dov Field
1516–1726	69	1603	Noach Maseng Bresslof Weissbrod	attack El Arish with 30*A50 bombs
			Ber Kahn Majzels Spicehandler	
			Swiel Jacobson	
1520–0741	3	0409	Front	Tel Nof Dov Field Tel Nof
1525–1700	101	2008/15	Cohen	escort Squadron 69
1525–1700	101	2004/14	Wilson	ditto

While the Battalion 82 task force was at nearby El Riah, Squadron 69 was tasked to bomb El Arish. Despite AAA damage suffered by two of the bombers during the same day's morning mission, all three B-17s

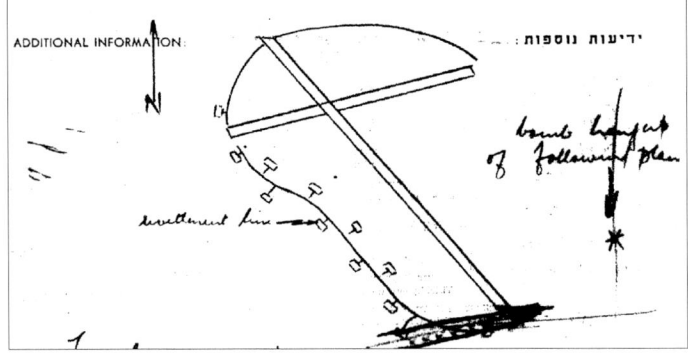

Squadron 69 bombed El Arish, on 29 December 1948, regardless of bad weather, thanks to the superb navigation of lead navigator John Harris. The bombing pattern scheme, from Raisin crew debrief, reveals hits along the southern part of the air base. The dot next to the bombing pattern is marked 'bomb hang up of following plane' but Feldman reported 'no hang ups' and Noach stated 'six overshoots'. Feldman's tail gunner Joe Lazarus reported 'no kites in revetments'.

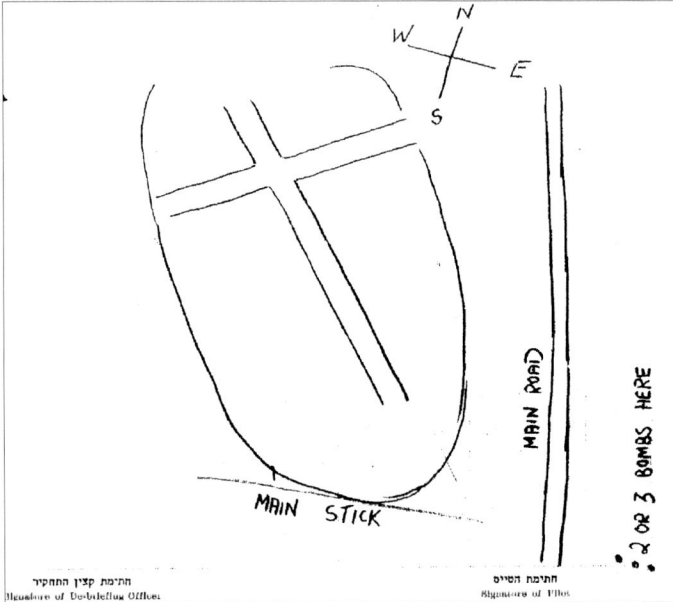

Squadron 101 pilots Sid Cohen and Denny Wilson illustrated observation of Squadron 69 bombing El Arish airfield in this sketch. The bombs seen to explode beyond target were probably Noach crew's overshoot.

were flying again. A probable AAA damage impact was the inclusion of gunner George Meyerson in the crews of both 1601 and 1602; it is likely that Meyerson actually flew in the latter B-17, replacing Wilfred Jackson who was injured during the morning mission.

The target, El Arish airfield, was the principal EGAF air base in north-east Sinai from May 1948, but by December it was no longer the center of EGAF operations over the battlefield, as already speculated in the Squadron 69 debrief report after the 26 December mission.

The lead bomber was over the target from 1612 until 1635, with the two wingmen over the target from 1635 until 1635. AAA fire was reportedly inaccurate and the major difficulty was cloudy weather and poor visibility. Leader flew two bombing runs. The description of the first run was:

> Whole area completely covered [with clouds], no bombs dropped.

The trio then returned at 15,000 feet for a live bombing run. The crew of 1603 stated:

> Target found due to SUPERB navigation by lead navigator [John Harris].

Squadron 101 pilots Sid Cohen and Denny Wilson were tasked to escort the bombers, as indicated in their debrief:

> Rendezvous at Nebi Rubin with three Hammers. Out over sea, south-west, broke land west of El Arish. Did one run west to east over target while 9/10 cloud over target. Second run from west to east and bombed through clouds. Main stick fell south of long runway. Flak, white and black, fair amount and accurate from 12,000 feet up to 17,000 feet. Bombed at 1635. Left them at 1645 and Hammers headed for home.

OBSERVATION JUDEA

1531–1643   3   0114   Ruff   observation Judea

The daily Squadron 3 scan of the Judea situation produced the following ILAFI report:

> Visibility was poor to bad. In Hirbet Sika observed about 30 Bedouin tents, refugees? At... Hirbet Weibda there is a concentration of about 40 to 50 refugee tents. In Dahariya... stone road blocks were observed and an Egyptian vehicle, which was traveling through them and proceeding northwards, fired a few shots at the aircraft. West of Dahariya... a caravan of six camels, loaded with boxes as well as three people, traveling north-west... Over Faluja tracers were encountered.

RAID BIR HAMA

1540–1630   101   2301/40   Augarten   patrol north-east Sinai
1540–1630   101   2302/41   Doyle   ditto

Squadron 101 pilots Rudy Augarten and Jack Doyle monitored the situation in north-east Sinai, as ILAFI reported:

> Visibility was poor. A field piece, firing south, was observed near the small field south of El Arish... The three Spitfires were observed, still in pens, and a Jeep was seen traveling on runway. At... about 20 vehicles... scattered on both sides of the road. At... a total of about 80 vehicles... scattered on both sides on the road. On the main road... a convoy of about 20 vehicles... Some pulling field pieces and heading north. Encountered both heavy and light ack ack at El Arish.

ILDF Front D Commander Yigal Alon visited El Riah during the afternoon hours of 29 December 1948.

Who is who was certainly difficult to ascertain and, luckily to all concerned, the P-51 pilots did not attack anything since, at that time, the Battalion 82 task force was in control of El Riah airfield where, around that time, Front D Commander Yigal Alon was visiting the forces at the frontline.

Meanwhile, the Battalion 7 task group raided Bir Hama from 1615. At the start of the attack, all resident aircraft, except for two, took off. Defense was much stiffer than expected and the Battalion 7 task group retreated without actually occupying Bir Hama.

END OF DAY 7

1646–1702	3	0106	Moller	test
2225–2354	3	0106	Biram	direct searchlights over Faluja
2345–0125	1	1306	Kaplan	Dov Field Ramat David Dov Field

ILAFI issued, at 1800, an end-of-day report that summed up enemy air activity as follows:

> Most of the tactical air activity centered about the Abu Ageila [to] El Arish area. Enemy planes dashed in from time to time to make passes at our ground forces but would make-off on the arrival of our own craft. There is a report of planes bearing the Iraqi triangular insignia appearing over the Negev Front. This report has not been confirmed.

The Israeli invasion of Egyptian territory in Sinai was aimed to force Egyptian forces to retreat from Palestine, but this objective was not accomplished yet, while the presence of Israeli forces in Sinai prompted nations to act, as indicated in a USA State Department report:

> British Embassy has just informed [USA State] Department as follows. British Foreign Office has received two cables from British Embassy Cairo dated 29 December [1948]. First quoted [Egypt War Minister] Haidar Pasha... as stating Israeli forces were in vicinity of Auja and some perhaps crossed Egyptian frontier. Message stated Egyptians were requesting UK permission for Egyptian Spitfires to operate out of Suez Canal zone.

Second and subsequent message quoted Haidar Pasha:

> Israelis were within 10 miles of El Arish and well over Egyptian frontier. British Foreign Office desired substance these two messages be given [USA State] Department. Foreign Office stated no confirmation from other sources but RAF had been instructed to verify by reconnaissance. If Israelis had in fact crossed Egyptian frontier, UK obligations under terms [of] Anglo-Egyptian treaty would of course come into play. [FRUS].

Bonded to Egypt in treaty and seemingly hostile to Israel, the UK promoted a UN Security Council resolution to which USA Special Representative in Israel James McDonald referred in a message from Tel Aviv on 29 December 1948:

> Acceptance by [UN] Security Counsel [sic]of... [British] resolution would, we believe, postpone peace in Negev by encouraging Egypt's continued refusal [to] negotiate armistice. Moreover, Israel cannot surrender military gains in Negev especially since Egypt shows no willingness [to] recognize Israel's existence... or to deal with Israel. [FRUS]

The UK-promoted proposition was duly accepted by the evening of 29 December – by a majority of eight votes to none, with the USA, USSR and Ukraine abstaining – as UN Security Council Resolution 66 (1948) states:

> The Security Council, having considered the report of the Acting Mediator on the hostilities which broke out in southern Palestine on 22 December 1948, calls upon the Governments concerned:
> (i) To order an immediate ceasefire;
> (ii) To implement without further delay resolution 61 (1948) of 4 November 1948 and the instructions issued by the Acting Mediator in accordance with sub paragraph (1) of the fifth paragraph of that resolution;
> (iii) To allow and facilitate the complete supervision of the truce by the UN observers;
> Instructs the committee of the Council appointed on 4 November [1948] to meet at Lake Success on 7 January 1949 to consider the situation in southern Palestine and to report to the Council on the extent to which the Governments concerned have by that date complied with the present resolution and with resolutions 61 (1948) and 62 (1948) of 4 and 16 November 1948. [FRUS]

Meanwhile, the ILDF and ILAF prepared for HOREV Day 8. Squadron 3 Auster 0106 was tasked to coordinate ILDF searchlights over the Faluja Pocket, as ILAFI reported:

> Visibility was good. Observed a number of explosions in Faluja. On reaching target (Faluja), searchlights were contacted by walkie talkie... and setting started. As soon as lights were fixed on target, our troops fired a number of bursts

ILAFI reported in November 1948 that Iraq deployed to Egypt three Fury fighters in return for Egypt supplying weapons to Iraq in order to arm Fury fighters that the UK delivered without weapons in order to comply with the UN embargo; this photo of an Iraqi Fury was reportedly taken during detachment to Egypt.

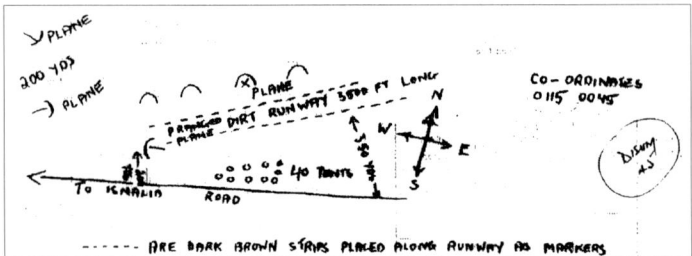

Squadron 101 pilots Augarten and Peake produced this sketch of Bir Hama airfield as observed on the morning of 30 December 1948, including sighting of a pranged fighter, perhaps one of the EGAF aircraft that Squadron 101 pilots engaged over Faluja on 28 December 1948.

DAY 8
30 DECEMBER 1948

Israel viewed UN Security Council Resolution 66 (1948) as a negative diplomatic development aimed to annihilate Israeli military accomplishments, but the fledgling State was not interested in a conflict with a world power.

HOREV did not yet accomplish the objective of defeating the EGDF in Israel; the ILDF indeed penetrated Sinai but Brigade 1's effort in the Gaza to Rafah sector failed and Brigade 3's attack against the Faluja Pocket was defeated. Israel, therefore, wished to press ahead with HOREV while avoiding conflict with the UK; how to accomplish this compound objective was the subject of an early morning discussion between ILPM David Ben-Gurion, ILDF Chief of Staff Jacob Dori, ILDF Deputy Chief of Staff Yigael Yadin and Front D Commander Yigal Alon. The meeting concluded with a decision to continue HOREV; to divert its main effort to the Gaza to Rafah sector; to attack El Arish from Abu Ageila as a diversion; to retreat to the international border if British armed forces arrived; and to fight the British armed forces if these crossed the international border from Egypt to Israel.

Accordingly, the ILDF issued OPOR HOREV Phase 2; the main objective was to force the EGDF to retreat from the Gaza Strip. In order to accomplish this objective, it planned to attack El Arish and Rafah and to insert a wedge between Gaza and Rafah. ILAF missions were defined as:

- Patrol enemy territory over Rafah and El Arish and over roads from Abu Ageila to El Arish, and from Abu Ageila to Ismailia.
- Secure our ground forces and operate against enemy aircraft over these sectors.

OBSERVATION BIR HAMA

0303–09:30	106	RX-136	Applebaum	VELVETTA 2 Tel Nof Niksic observation
0540–0700	2	Piper	Eyal	observation
0719–0846	101	2301/40	Augarten	observation north-east Sinai
0719–0846	101	2302/41	Peake	ditto

Augarten and Peake were the first ILAF pilots to fly over the new Bir Hama airfield; they reported poor visibility, no AAA fire and no enemy aircraft in the air, as indicated in the debrief report:

> Went first to [Bir Hama] field... Then went back to small field south of El Arish but saw no activity there or in fields around or on road to El Arish. El Arish itself obscured by rain. Flew out to sea, came back in east of Bir Burg... and observed train... Strafed train and made a total of seven passes at train. Observed strikes on engine and cars; six or eight passenger coaches in train. Train was proceeding south from Rafah to El Arish and was eventually brought to stop after rolling three kilometres. Truck on highway also stopped...

Tel Nof - formerly RAF Station Aqir - was the largest ILAF air base at the time, hosting Squadron 3, Squadron 106, Flight 35 and Air Maintenance Unit; VELVETTA 2 Spitfires landed at Tel Nof after Squadron 106 C-46's lead ship returned to its home base in order to be inspected by the Air Maintenance Unit prior to issue to Squadron 101 at Hatzor.

VELVETTA 2 FLIGHT 3

0730–	3	0114	Ruff	Tel Nof Dov Field Beer Sheba Dov Field Hatzor Beer Sheba Dov Field Tel Nof training
0855–1000	3	0407	Biram	training
0930–1030	2	Piper	Eyal	Beer Sheba Dov Field Beer Sheba
0949–1035	3	0409	Dankner	training
1000–1615	106	RX-130	Ford Bradshaw Story	VELVETTA 2 Niksic Tel Nof leader
1000–1605	101	2019	Schroeder	VELVETTA 2 Niksic Tel Nof
1000–1610	101	2015	Jacobs	VELVETTA 2 Niksic Tel Nof
1000–1635	106	RX-137	Keren	VELVETTA 2 Niksic Tel Nof trailer

The last two of the 12 VELVETTA 2 Spitfires flew from Yugoslavia to Israel in good weather, in an uneventful trip, trailing behind Squadron 106 RX-130 at 9,000 to 10,000 feet. Thus ended delivery of 12 Spitfires that were originally planned to arrive before the start of HOREV; of the 12 Spitfires that arrived from HOREV Day 1 to Day 8, only three – 2008, 2012 and 2018 – were operational with Squadron 101 by the time 2015 and 2019 landed at Tel Nof.

RX-137 trailed as rearguard and also transported cargo from Niksic to Tel Nof. Post-landing, RX-137 crew complained that aircraft demonstrated heaviness during flight and it turned out that it was loaded with 4,130 kilograms of cargo while the recommended load for C-46 flight from Niksic to Tel Nof was 2,800 kilograms.

COMBAT OVER ABU AGEILA

| 1003–1124 | 101 | 2004/14 | Doyle | patrol north-east Sinai |
| 1003–1124 | 101 | 2008/15 | McElroy | ditto |

Squadron 101 pilots Jack Doyle and John McElroy reported very good visibility, monitored Bir Hama, patrolled over El Arish and engaged enemy aircraft over Abu Ageila, as described in their debrief:

> Flew down to Bir Hama. No activity from FIATs on drome. No variance from first patrols observations. Observed white vehicle with men jumping into it. At least 30 stationary vehicles on the field. Back from Bir Hama along main road to within six miles of Abu Ageila, then north to main road Abu Ageila to El Arish... [At] small field south of El Arish... one Spit sitting in open. A little north of small field sighted two FIATs. Chased them, unobserved by them. Climbed into sun [and] caught them in their strafing run after they had dropped bombs on Abu Ageila, right on bridge and crossroads; could not observe extent of damage. Doyle engaged Number 1 FIAT from his starboard quarter. Close in line 200 yards astern. Fired short bursts. Observed strikes, black smoke and glycol poured out and he went starboard going down. Did not see aircraft crash. Broke up port when signaled by our [Number] 2 Spit. Covered [Number] 2 Spit while he hacked away at second FIAT. McElroy attacked second FIAT as it was pulling up from strafing run. Closed on his tail to 400 yards, climbing from deck, firing burst continually through violent evasive action. No strikes till FIAT got on Doyle's tail. Fired three seconds burst, FIAT broke to port leaving Doyle. Continued dogfight till FIAT started to pour white smoke and went down south in a shallow dive. Broke off combat. In opinion of both pilots, FIAT is highly maneuverable. Enemy pilots' action during combat denote high combat experience.

None of the engaged enemy aircraft was seen to crash. ILAFI Condensed Operational Summary Number 7, for the timeframe from 1900 on 29 December until 1900 on 30 December, reported:

> Two Enemy FIATs were downed by two of our Spitfires in a dogfight over Abu Ageila.

But a Front D report from 2130 stated:

> Enemy aircraft bombed our forces in the Auja to Abu Ageila [sector] throughout the day. Damages were light. One enemy aircraft was hit and was seen to fly away pouring smoke.

While an end-of-day Israel Ministry for Foreign Affairs Press and Information Division Press Release Number 2 stated:

> An Israeli military spokesman announced this evening that two Egyptian aircraft of the FIAT type were shot down this afternoon in the Negev.

This was an inaccurate statement, since air combat was in the late morning hours over Sinai and not in the afternoon over Negev.

The ILAF transformed reported hits into confirmed kills and credited Doyle and McElroy with one kill each.

OBSERVATION JUDEA

1015–	2	0408	Cohen	observation north-east Sinai
1024–1310	3	0405	Navot	observation Judea
1029–1051	3	0407	Lee	training
1055–1115	1	0412	Efrat Porat	training

Squadron 3 pilot Nathan Navot was tasked to fly the daily inspection of activity in the Judea sector, as ILAFI reported:

> Visibility was medium. At Iraq Manshiya... 17 vehicles near the village. In the northern portion of town... vehicles camouflaged among trees, near gun positions. In Faluja/Beit Sika area, a tractor, people moving and two to three camels led by civilians... The area south of Sika is full of Bedouin tents. At Idna, three civilian vehicles and a gathering of people... West of Tarqumiya, a double road block... At... a stone house surrounded by well-camouflaged tents... with camouflaged trenches in the surroundings... From village of Dir Nakhas there is a grade B road leading to above-mentioned concentration. From the concentration to two dominating heights... a grade B road... with vehicles' tracks on it. From Beit Jibrin/Tarqumiya road a mountain track leads to above-mentioned concentration also. The track itself is defended by trenches. At... on Beit Jibrin/Tarqumiya road there is an anti-tank barricade which stretches across the width of the valley. The block is constructed of iron Xs (hedgehog).

RAID FALUJA

A group of Flying School advance training cadets assigned to Squadron 3 at Tel Nof for the duration of HOREV. From left to right, from top to bottom: Katriel Greenspan, Nathan Navot, Shaya Gazit, Isaac Volowitz, Azriel Ronen, Gershon Lee, Abraham Yoffe and Meir Ruff.

1133–1202	35	1106	Gibson	attack Faluja with 8*50kg bombs
1133–1202	35	1102	Dougherty	ditto
1133–1202	35	1105	Flint	ditto
1133–1202	35	1107	Brown	ditto

Flight 35 was over the Faluja Pocket from 1150 to 1151. Pilots reported poor visibility, attacked artillery emplacements and reported hits.

PATROL NORTH-EAST SINAI

1140–1450	1	0602	Solarsh	Dov Field Haifa Ramat David Dov Field
1204–1326	3	0409	Dankner	Tel Nof Dov Field Tel Nof
1320–1625	1	0412	Ospovat	Dov Field Beer Sheba Dov Field
1357–1525	101	2004/14	Weizman	patrol north-east Sinai
1400–1525	101	2008/15	Ruch	ditto

Squadron 101 pilots Ezer Weizman and Arnold Ruch patrolled the HOREV theater of operations, as ILAFI reported:

> Visibility... was fair. Observed nothing on El Arish road but observed what appeared to be 20 stationary vehicles on the road near El Arish field. Heavy vehicular traffic on Rafah/El Arish road. Aircraft made four passes at a truck and three Bren carriers (or possibly half-tracks) and observed strikes and smoke arising from one Bren carrier. Three others turned around and went back towards Rafah.

FETCH SPITFIRE FROM EL RIAH

1410–1600	2	Piper	Portugali	Beer Sheba AbuAgeila Beer Sheba
1419–1433	3	0409	Katzin	training
1430–1538	3	0110	Biram	training
1440–1803	3	0106	Navot	Tel Nof Dov Field Tel Nof
1450–1705	1	0702	Kaplan	Dov Field Ramat David Tel Nof Dov Field
1500–1645	1	0602	Solarsh	Dov Field Hatzor Dov Field
1528–1647	101	0419	Axelrod	Hatzor Tel Nof Hatzor
1533–0812	3	0409	Dankner	Tel Nof Dov Field Tel Nof

Front D reported the capture of a seemingly-intact Spitfire at El Riah, so ILAF Operations Chief David Judah ordered Squadron 101 to dispatch a Spitfire pilot to El Riah for an attempt to fly it from there. Squadron 3 pilot Meir Ruff flew Squadron 101 pilot Boris Senior, in Auster 0114, from Hatzor to Beer Sheba, while Squadron 2 pilot Abraham Portugali flew Senior, in a Piper, from Beer Sheba to Abu Ageila. Simultaneously, ILAF Operations Chief Deputy Dan Tolkowsky, Squadron 2 Operations Officer Hanoch Wislitsky and a technical team in a truck arrived at Abu Ageila. The team departed Abu Ageila for El Riah, with an escort of three Jeeps, circa 1500 or later.

All efforts to start the engine of the Spitfire failed and it was towed from El Riah to Abu Ageila, where the tail section was lightly damaged

An Egyptian Spitfire dummy - with EGAF Number 608 – which the ILDF captured at El Riah.

The captured EGAF Number 664 Spitfire during tow, as photographed by a British reconnaissance aircraft - most likely along the road from El Riah to Abu Ageila - on 30 December 1948.

during unloading and the technical team dismantled vital parts – two guns and ammunition, four machine guns and ammunition, sight, battery, radio and mirror. The dismantled Spitfire was placed under a camouflage net at Abu Ageila and the three pilots and technical team returned to Beer Sheba with the dismantled parts.

BIR HAMA STATUS REPORT

1550–1700	101	2301/40	Cohen	patrol north-east Sinai
1550–1700	101	2302/41	Goodlin	ditto
1640–1707	3	0110	Moller	training
1641–1700	3	0405	Rosen	training

At 16:00, OWL HQ reported:

> A long column of armor and Bren carries from Rafah to El Arish. Nearly no movement along all other roads. Four sorties attacked column [from Rafah to El Arish]. Reported hits. Two more aircraft dispatched to engage this column.

Squadron 101 pilots Syd Cohen and Slick Goodlin reported visibility as fair to poor and still noted the captured Spitfire at El Riah, but did not attack the aforementioned column between Rafah and El Arish, as indicated in the debrief report:

> Proceeded direct to Auja, then to Abu Ageila, then ordered by Tel Nof tower to Abu Ageila/Rafah road for reported bandits [enemy aircraft] but did not find any. Observed fairly heavy traffic towards El Arish on Rafah/El Arish road. In field, south

of El Arish field, observed the Spitfire previously reported. Then proceeded to Abu Ageila and then west on Ismailia road... [to] airfield at Bir Hama. At this airfield, observed at least six single-engine aircraft, four of which were in pens; one of the aircraft appeared to be white. South-east of field is a camp with at least 30 tents.

EVENING BOMBINGS

1705–1930	103	1401	Katz Nathan Festing Pozkanzner attack Faluja with 16★A100 kg bombs
1720–1920	103	1405	Rosin Agmon Laron Manor attack Faluja with 16★A100 kg bombs
2240–0015	103	1401	Katz Nathan Festing Pozkanzner attack Faluja with 8★100kg bombs+ Hollander Berger Pinto 8★30kg+30★3kg incendiary bombs
2325–0022	106	RX-133	Lewis attack Gaza with 24★50kg+AI3 bombs
2335–0110	103	1405	Rosin Agmon Laron Manor attack Faluja with 8★100kg bombs+ Erlich 8★30kg+25★3kg incendiary bombs

Squadron 103's 1401 crew reported fair weather and good visibility over the target; they were over Faluja from 1755 until 1820 and flew three bombing runs at 4,500 feet, as indicated in their debrief:

> Run 1... direction east to west, four bombs dropped, fell in northern sector of town, near road...
> Run 2... approximately south-east to north-west, six bombs dropped between main road and airfield perimeter track, appeared to fell in sandy area.
> Run 3... north-east to south-west, remaining six bombs dropped, hit in south-west corner of airfield perimeter track, normal bomb explosions.
> Over again, army failed to supply searchlights as promised; extremely difficult to locate exact target area.

Squadron 103's 1405 crew also reported fair weather and good visibility over the target, was over Faluja from 1830 until 1831 and flew one bombing run at 4,000 feet, as indicated in the debrief:

> Arrived at target early so circled at 5,000 feet awaiting other aircraft to bomb first. First stick of other aircraft almost hit plane so flew and circled vicinity of Majdal. Called up other plane on radio, told him that we were going to bomb as he had lost target.
> One run [heading] 120... bombs straddle target between center and south of town as briefed. Normal explosions, no fires. Left target, circled and observed bombing of second aircraft.
> As crossed coastline, heading homeward, army KINDLY put on searchlight for plane, searchlight from Hulikat, very strong searchlight; unfortunately, a little too late... Entire coast has poor blackout, NEW YEAR LIGHTS?

Squadron 103's 1401 crew returned for a second bombing of Faluja from 2325 until 2336, flying two bombing runs at 4,000 feet,

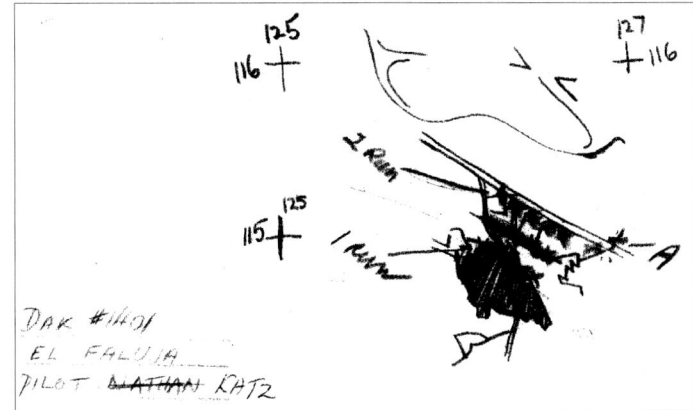

A debrief sketch illustrating Squadron 103 C-47 1401's second bombing sortie over Faluja during the night of 30 to 31 December 1948.

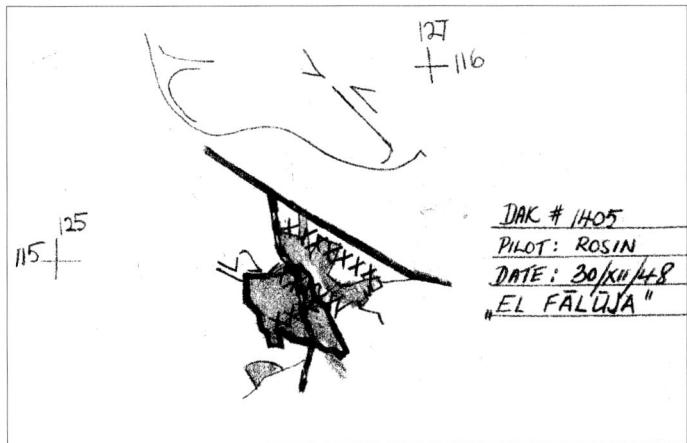

Squadron 103 C-47 1405 flew three bombing runs over Faluja during the second bombing sortie on the night of 30 to 31 December 1948, as this debrief sketch illustrates.

reporting good weather and good visibility over target, as indicated in their debrief:

> Saw two beautiful searchlights crossing over Faluja...
> Run 1 [heading] 110. Dropped eight 30 kilograms incendiaries and 15 three kilograms incendiaries. Direct hit was scored in north sector of town. Beside secondary explosions and fire, saw one large building (wooden evidently from rate of fire) completely burning.
> Run 2 [heading] 110. Dropped eight 100 kilograms bombs plus 14 three kilograms incendiaries. Stick fell north of first stick. Two fires started, one south and one north of road on east outskirts of town... Target... was definitely hit and result of mission could not have been achieved without army searchlights.

Squadron 106's RX-133 was over Gaza from 2350 until 0001 but did not bomb, as ILAFI reported:

> Visibility was very bad. Bombs could not be dropped over target because of 10/10ths cloud condition and they were, therefore, jettisoned at sea.

Squadron 103's 1405 crew returned for a second bombing of Faluja from 0020 until 0029, flying three bombing runs at 3,000 feet, reporting fair weather and fair to dark visibility over the target, as indicated in the debrief:

Run 1 [heading] 090. Released all 30 kilograms and 100 kilograms. Bombs straddled north center of town. One large fire... One large explosion.

Run 2 [heading] 090. Released 10 incendiaries. Parallel to first run and to south of it...

Run 3 [heading] 200. Searchlights came on for this run. Last three incendiaries dropped across center of town...

Three fires seen on southern perimeter of [Faluja] airfield... searchlights put on too late.

END OF DAY 8

British aircraft, in coordination with the EGAF, flew a reconnaissance mission over north-east Sinai on 30 December. This mission confirmed that the ILDF indeed penetrated Sinai, and UK Ambassador passed this information to USA Acting Secretary of State, as FRUS indicated:

> The British Ambassador... read... reports from the British Ambassador in Cairo to the effect that an Israeli column had bifurcated in vicinity of Beer Sheba and that attacks were being made by Israeli forces across Egyptian frontier from south and south-east on a line from Rafah extending 15 kilometers in direction of El Arish. One Egyptian airstrip on Egyptian territory had been taken by the Israeli forces. Egyptian Spitfires had landed out of gas on British airfields in the [Suez] Canal zones, thus implying that advanced Egyptian airfields were no longer operable.

Consequently, the UK delivered to the USA a Note Verbale:

> All the evidence in possession of the British Government points to the fact that, notwithstanding the truce and the resolutions passed by the UN, Israeli forces are fighting on Egyptian territory, where they are in possession of airfields... The British Government regard the situation with grave concern. Unless the Jews withdraw from Egyptian territory, the British Government will be bound to take steps to fulfill their obligations under their treaty of 1936 with Egypt... The British Government have no desire to get into conflict with the Jews... They trust that it will be possible for the US Government so to act upon the Jews as to make any military action by British forces on Egyptian territory unnecessary under our treaty with Egypt. This can only be ensured if the Jews immediately withdraw from Egyptian territory. Meanwhile, the British Government feel bound to take the necessary steps to protect their own troops and installations in Transjordan... In view of the very serious danger, the British Government must now proceed to move equipment into Transjordan. Moreover, in view of the aggressive use to which the Jews have put arms obtained from Russian satellite countries, the British Government will find themselves in a position in which they are no longer able to refuse to carry out British contracts to the Arab countries.[FRUS]

The British reference to Israel as Jews – the same as the reference to Egypt as Muslims – highlighted the precarious position of the former empire, but the USA generously came to help its smaller and weaker ally; around midnight, USA Acting Secretary of State wired to The Special Representative of the USA in Israel, James McDonald:

Two Squadron 69 air gunners - Joe Lazarus (second from left) and Jack Gershaw (fourth from left) - and two Squadron 103 radio operators - Milton Boettger (third from left) and Phil Kemp (fifth from left) - offer a drink to Squadron 103 Commander Daniel Rosin (left) during a wedding at Haifa on 19 February 1949; Rosin flew two bombing missions in C-47 1405 on the evening of 30 December 1948.

The Special Representative of the USA in Israel, James Grover McDonald - the tall, older man in a civilian suit - visiting an ILAF exhibition later in 1949.

> President directs that you make following immediate representation to [ILFM] Shertok and [ILPM] Ben-Gurion... This Government is most deeply disturbed on receipt of apparently authentic reports confirming that Egyptian territory has been invaded by armed forces of Israel... British Government has officially notified this Government that it regards situation with grave concern and that unless Israeli forces withdraw from Egyptian territory, British Government will be bound to take steps to fulfill their obligations under Treaty of 1936 with Egypt... As first government to recognize Israel... this Government, with deep concern... draw attention of Israeli Government to grave possibility... of... a reconsideration by this Government of its relations with Israel... Immediate withdrawal of Israeli forces from Egyptian territory appears to be minimum requirement... if enlarged conflict is to be avoided... [FRUS]

DAY 9
31 DECEMBER 1948

The USA Special Representative in Israel, James McDonald, delivered the Anglo-American message to the ILFM on 31 December, but it was Friday and the ILPM was already at Tiberias for his regular weekend of spa.

RAID FALUJA

0330–0520	103	1401	Katz Nathan Festing Pozkanzner attack Faluja with 8*A100kg+8* AI30kg+31*AI3kg bombs Hollander Berger Pinto
0455–0625	103	1405	Rosin Agmon Laron Manor attack Faluja with 8*100kg+8* 30kg+25*AI3 bombs Erlich Stern Grunberger

The two Squadron 103 C-47 bombers each completed three bombing sorties over Faluja during the night of 30 to 31 December, by 0520 and 0625.

The 1401 crew reported good weather, very good visibility over the target, no AAA fire, TOT from 0415 until 0439 and bombing from 4,000 feet, as debriefed:

> Three runs over target area; each: direction 110.
> First run dropped eight 30-kilogram incendiary bombs plus 10 three-kilogram incendiaries. All bombs fell in northern center of town.
> Second run dropped eight 100-kilogram plus 13 AI3 bombs falling in same area, somewhat south...
> Third run balance of small incendiaries dropped. All bombs dropped close to searchlight intersection; 30-kilogram incendiaries seem to cause number of glowing points...
> All bombs fell very close to those dropped in second mission.

1405's crew reported good weather, good visibility over the target, no AAA fire, TOT from 0530 until 0540 and two bombing runs at 4,000 feet, as debriefed:

> First run [heading] 120. Half load dropped south sector of target. Normal explosions.
> Second run [heading] 150. Same result... Both searchlights well on.

The laconic report was excused by the debrief officer at the bottom of the debrief form:

> Lack of complete information due to crew's third night trip and being too tired to be cooperative.

ATTACK BIR HAMA

0530–0950	1	1306	Ospovat	Dov Field Tel Nof Sodom Dov Field
0530–1000	1	1305	Solarsh	Dov Field Tel Nof Sodom Dov Field
0600–0930	2	0403	Cohen	observation Auja Abu Ageila

The ILPM (and Defense Minister as well) David Ben-Gurion (left) - reviewing an ILDF parade with ILDF Chief of Staff Jacob Dori (right) - was deeply involved in the conduct of ILDF operations, but vacationed every weekend at Tiberias.

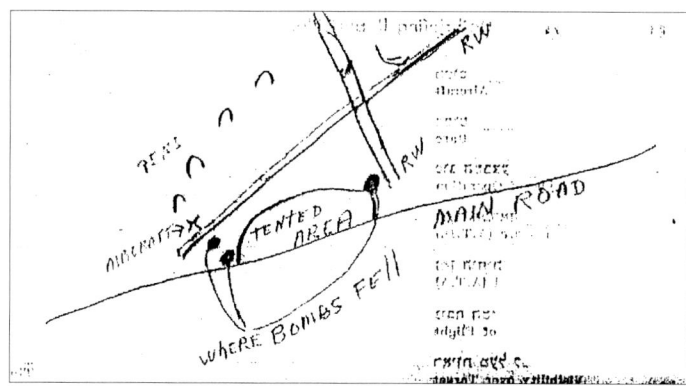

A Squadron 101 debrief sketch of Bir Hama after the raid on 31 December 1948; Syd Cohen, Denny Wilson and Jack Cohen also reported a seemingly damaged fighter nearby the south-east edge of the south-east north-west runway. The illustrated road is Abu Ageila Ismailia.

0630–1000	2	0401		observation Gaza Rafah
0657–1108	3	0114	Giladi	Tel Nof Dov Field Beer Sheba Tel Nof
0700–0945	1	1301	Kaplan	Dov Field Beer Sheba Dov Field
0700–0820		101	2003/12 Cohen	attack Bir Hama with 2*100lb bombs
0700–0820		101	2008/15 Wilson	ditto
0700–0820		101	2002/11 Cohen	ditto

The Battalion 7 task force's failure to raid Bir Hama on 29 December and continued EGAF operations from Bir Hama during 30 December prompted an ILAF raid on 31 December, as debriefed:

> Proceeded direct to Bir Hama airfield. Two Spitfires dive-bombed... At this time a FIAT was flying over airfield at about 2,000 feet. Wilson, who was in his dive at the time, dropped his bombs and got on the FIAT's tail. He opened fire and hit the

FIAT's starboard elevator. Fired approximately six bursts at the FIAT and observed strikes on each burst. The FIAT was seen by all of our planes to have spun in and crashed about six miles west of the field and then burned.

Syd Cohen made strafing passes. [First pass at] what appeared to be a damaged FIAT that was parked in the western side of the field area. On Syd Cohen's second pass, he strafed a FIAT that was taxiing in the north-western area of the field.

Jack Cohen and Denny Wilson both made one pass at the same damaged aircraft reported above.

There appeared to be three or four aircraft on the field and scattered vehicle movement on the field.

At El Arish observed approximately 40 to 50 vehicles of all description about one mile south of north-west [to] south-east runway. Low trajectory heavy flak from El Arish.

ILAFI Condensed Operational Summary Number 7 reported:

Two enemy FIATs were destroyed by our Spitfires at Bir Hama on 31 December [1948]. One of the FIATs was caught on the ground; the other was hit while in the air.

An Arab perspective narrative stated:

... during a large ILAF attack on the Bir Hama airstrip on 31 December [1948]... Mustafa Kamal Abed Wahab and... Khalaf Arusah, both said to be flying Macchis, were shot down and killed as they tried to take off. A third Macchi claimed by the Israelis was possibly damaged. [PXNE p116]

The ILAF credited Clifford Denzel Wilson with a kill.

OBSERVATION JUDEA

Time	Sqn	A/C	Pilot	Mission
0840–0945	1	0702	Efrat Lavi	training
0844–0943	3	0405	Front	training
0845–1030	2	Piper	Portugali	Beer Sheba Hatzor Beer Sheba
0911–1020	3	0407	Katzin	training
1025–1310	1	0702	Efrat	Dov Field Haifa Ramat David Tel Nof Dov Field
1043–1200	3	0409	Machnes	observation Judea
1100–	1	0602	Renov	Dov Field Tel Nof Hatzor Dov Field
1105–1229	3	0106	Front	Tel Nof Dov Field Tel Nof
1119–1331	3	0114	Rutevitz	Tel Nof Dov Field Tel Nof

Squadron 2 pilot Abraham Portugali returned Squadron 101 pilot Boris Senior from Beer Sheba to Hatzor, thus ending the latter's involvement in the attempt to retrieve the captured EGAF 664 Spitfire from El Riah. Squadron 3 pilot Benjamin Machnes – reassigned from Squadron 1 to Squadron 3 on 29 December – flew an observation mission over Judea, as ILAFI reported:

Visibility was good. Recced south of Faluja Pocket and found traces of the camel caravan captured on the night of 30 to 31 December [1948]. In the canyons at... three large Bedouin camps, each containing about 25 tents. Near... a few herds as well as three loaded camels and two donkeys...

ILAFI Condensed Operational Summary Number 7 also reported capture of the camel caravan:

A caravan on the way to Faluja from the Bet Lehem area was intercepted by our forces. The caravan consisted of 14 camels bearing ammunition, rifle oil, food stuffs, fuel, mail and newspapers.

RAID EL ARISH FALUJA

Time	Sqn	A/C	Crew	Mission
1130–1415	69	1601	Raisin Goldstein Harris Cuburnek Lichtman Goldstein Aronson Meyerson Duboff Gershaw Hill	attack El Arish with 16*100kg bombs diverted to attack Faluja
1132–1413	69	1603	Noach Maseng Bresslof Weissbrod Ber Majzels Kahn Spicehandler Swiel Jacobson	attack El Arish with 24*A100 bombs diverted to attack Faluja
1133–1432	69	1602	McConville Spink Seftel Weinstein Cohen Schwartzbach Christiensen Cohen Robinson Kaplan Liponetzky	attack El Arish with 16*100kg bombs diverted to attack Faluja
11:45–1300	1	0412	Solarsh Kraft	training
1154–1401	101	2008/15	Goodlin	escort Squadron 69
1154–1401	101	2012/16	Dangott	ditto

Squadron 69 was tasked to bomb the El Arish marshaling yards but the B-17 crews were unable to pinpoint the target due to clouds. The alternative target, Rafah, was also covered with clouds so the trio of bombers attacked Faluja. The 1601 crew was over Faluja from 1324 until 1327, reported visibility over the target of up to 20 miles, no AAA fire and bombing from 10,000 feet, as debriefed:

One run [heading] 096; bombs dropped across south edge of town. Direct hit on large house. Hits were scored on trenchwork. Friction between crew members as to where run was made... COMPLAINT: No adequate code system exists to ask for alternative target.

The 1603 crew was over Faluja from 1326 until 1326, reported good visibility over the target, no AAA fire and bombing from 10,000 feet, as debriefed:

Original target El Arish marshaling yard cloud cover 10/10; alternative target Rafah ditto; bombed Faluja. One run [heading] 095...

The 1602 crew was over Faluja from 1325 until 1332, reported fair weather, good visibility over the target, no AAA fire and bombing from 8,000 feet, as debriefed:

10/10 cloud at El Arish, proceeded Majdal, then Faluja. At Faluja had 100 per cent hang-up. Electrical circuit – cause. Bombs brought back to base, unable to jettison. Suggest

DAY 9: 31 DECEMBER 1948

weather flight made by single-engine aircraft half an hour before take-off.

Squadron 101 pilots Slick Goodlin and Caesar Dangott appear to have not been informed of 1602's hang-up so interpreted its behavior in a different manner:

The B-17 1602 returned to Ramat David with bombs on 31 December 1948 after flying to El Arish and then attempting to bomb Faluja. Bomb hang-ups were common during Squadron 69 missions, but B-17 crews mostly managed to jettison the objector weapons prior to return to base, but not that time.

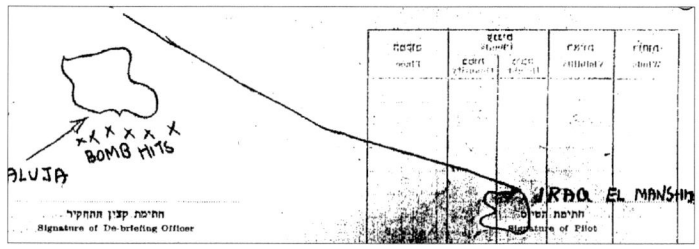

Squadron 101 pilots produced this sketch of the Squadron 69 Faluja bombing on 31 December 1948 - stating that bombs fell one mile south of Faluja.

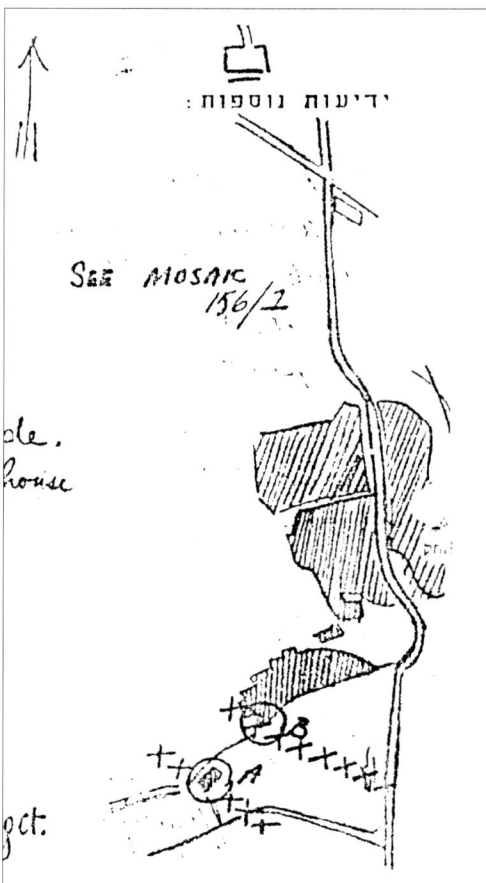

The Squadron 69 B-17 1601 crew debrief included this sketch of the Faluja bombing with two optional patterns of the same bombing run due to: Two divided opinions whether house... A or B, this would alter bombing accordingly.

Rendezvous with Forts [over] Nebi Rubin. Forts five minutes ahead of schedule. Direct over sea to El Arish. El Arish clouded over. Circles area but cloud was 10/10. Flew north to coast off Majdal. Made several circles while waiting for cloud cover over Faluja to move or to receive further instructions. After about one hour, orbit off coast of Majdal, before [B-17s] making run over Faluja, [Spitfires] made one run each. Cleared target and flew out to sea. One B-17 broke and made what appeared to be a photo run of Faluja area. Then this B-17 flew out to sea, north about 10 miles, saw no more of him. Due to lack of fuel, Spits returned to base.

COULD NOT SEE SPITFIRE

1255–1620	1	1305	Kaplan	Dov Field Tel Nof Sodom Dov Field
1310–1630	1	1306	Steinman	Dov Field Tel Nof Sodom Dov Field
1320–1630	2	Piper	Eyal	Beer Sheba Dov Field Beer Sheba
1326–1458	101	2001/10	Senior	patrol north-east Sinai
1326–1458	101	2003/12	McElroy	ditto

Squadron 1 Rapides again supplied Sodom and Squadron 101 Spitfires once more patrolled north-east Sinai; pilots Boris Senior and John McElroy debriefed:

Flew down over Auja. Observed small cloud of white smoke... which thought to be bomb blast but no trace of aircraft; smoke disappeared quickly. Then down over main road to Abu Ageila.

The captured Spitfire EGAF Number 664 under a camouflage net outside Abu Ageila, nearby Ruefa Dam; the Spitfire blended in with its surroundings so well that even Boris Senior, who was present when it was camouflaged, was unable to spot it from the air.

Barely visible, due to camouflaging, is the tail section of the captured Spitfire EGAF Number 664 that was damaged during unloading at Abu Ageila.

Fairly well-dispersed transport off the road, could not see [captured EGAF 664] Spitfire [that Boris Senior left] parked between [Ruefa] Dam and Abu Ageila. Over to Bir Hama, no transport on road [from Abu Ageila to Bir Hama] and none on road [from Bir Hama] to Ismailia for 20 kilometers. At Bir Hama saw one aircraft evidently crashed over the side of runway; no others in pens; no activity and no flak at Bir Hama... Back up to main road Abu Ageila to El Arish. Observed 30-plus vehicles well-dispersed on either side of road about five to 10 kilometers south of El Arish. Encountered flak there. Saw no transport on main road between dispersion south of El Arish and Abu Ageila. Over to Gvulot by way of Auja/Rafah road. Observed six to eight vehicles heading towards Rafah from Auja about halfway along road. Then to Gvulot. From there to Khan Yunes. Between Dir Balah and Gaza saw about 10 vehicles (Jeeps?) going both ways. No observation to be made at Gaza field. Then proceeded home.

BIR HAMA EVACUATION?

1346–1621	3	0407	Simantov	Tel Nof Haifa Tel Nof
1357 –17:20	3	0114	Roth	Tel Nof (Dov Field) Tel Nof
1435–1507	3	0405	Navot Lee	training
1445–1610	1	0702	Solarsh Lavi	test and training
1445–1630	1	0603	Renov	Dov Field Ramat David Dov Field
1510–1755	1	0412	Efrat Porat	Dov Field Beer Sheba Dov Field
1510–0805	3	0106	Biram	Tel Nof Dov Field Tel Nof
1515–1617	3	0405	Zavadi	training
1525–1649	101	2012/16)	Augarten	patrol north-east Sinai
1532–1649	101	2008/15	Feldman	ditto

ILDF Day 9 activity was limited in scale, as ILAFI Condensed Operational Summary Number 7 indicated:

> Most of the action of the past few days has been of a limited nature. Our troops in the Negev continue to consolidate their newly-won positions and to patrol surrounding areas. A mobile force raided Bir Hasana [some 60 kilometers south-west of Abu Ageila and circa 30 kilometers south-east of Bir Hama]... 200 prisoners were taken, including 12 officers.

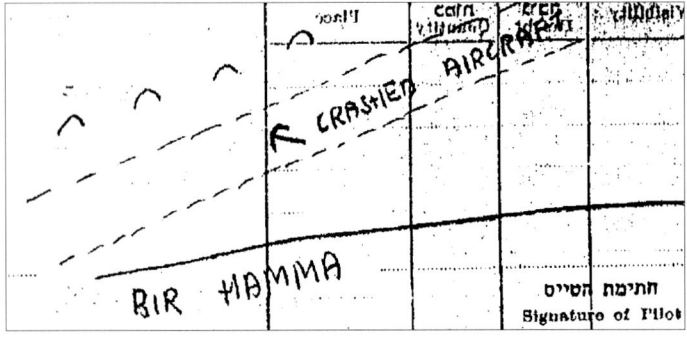

Squadron 101 pilots Senior and McElroy sighted a crashed aircraft roughly midway along the Bir Hama runway; was it the damaged aircraft that was previously spotted at the south-west side of the runway? Was it the taxiing aircraft strafed during the morning raid? Was it deliberately placed at the middle of the runway as an element of the EGAF evacuation of Bir Hama?

Squadron 101 pilots Rudy Augarten and Seymour Feldman monitored activity in the HOREV sector, as ILAFI reported:

> Visibility was fair. Observed nothing at Abu Ageila and a few vehicles at Bir Hama heading towards Ismailia. At Bir Hama, observed a very large fire with 20-feet flames and black smoke. A concentration of 40 to 50 vehicles was seen at... They were fairly widely dispersed (60 yards between vehicles). Another concentration, larger than above mentioned, was seen at... Nothing observed south of the concentration on main road from El Arish to Abu Ageila until about four to five miles north of Abu Ageila, where several vehicles traveling in both directions were observed. Little or no movement and no trains... between El Arish and Rafah and nothing... within a radius of four miles off the coast. At El Arish medium ack ack was encountered... and off the coast at Gaza heavy, fairly accurate ack ack...

This report indicates the EGAF's evacuation of Bir Hama air base.

SQUADRON 106 MISCONDUCT

1535–1645	1	1302	Solarsh Avisar	test and training
1632–1640	101	2013/18	Cohen	Tel Nof Hatzor delivery to Squadron 101
1703–1835	1	0602	Renov	Dov Field Tel Nof Hatzor Dov Field

The ILFM notified the ILPM, in a phone call to Tiberias, at noon, about the Anglo-American ultimatum and about the USA Special Representative in Israel James McDonald's intention to travel to Tiberias in order to deliver a message to the ILPM. The agreed course of action was to retreat from Sinai in order to avoid conflict with the UK and to continue action against the Gaza Strip and Faluja Pocket in order to accomplish the original objective of HOREV.

Previously, the ILAF already planned to bomb Gaza and Faluja during the night of 31 December 1948 to 1 January 1949. Squadron 103 was tasked to bomb Faluja and Squadron 106 was to bomb Gaza with TOT from 1800. Circa 1420, Squadron 106 notified the ILAF that it was impossible to assemble two C-46 crews for night-time missions due to the reported illness of many crew members though, obviously, the true reason was unwillingness to miss the New Year party! Two makeshift crews were duly assembled but the original TOT had to be delayed.

RAID GAZA FALUJA

1652–1817	103	1405	Orringer Keidar Weinstein Kemp	attack Faluja with 8*A100+8*AI30 bombs
1700–1830	103	1401	Shatkai Boshes Millman Boettger	attack Faluja with 8*100kg+8*AI30 bombs
1820–1923	3	0409	Front	weather observation Gaza
2020–2225	1	0602	Solarsh	Dov Field Ramat David Dov Field
2105–2340	106	RX-131	Bradshaw Foster	attack Gaza with 24*A50+AI3 bombs
2109–2251	103	1405	Orringer Keidar Weinstein Kemp	

			attack Faluja with 8*A100+8*AI30+ Hollander Stern Berger 25*3kg incendiary bombs
21 50–2345	103	1401	Boshes Shatkai Millman Boettger attack Faluja with 8*100kg+8*30kg bombs
2210–2335	106	RX-137	Henenson Tal attack Gaza with 24*A50+AI3 bombs

The 1405 crew was over Faluja from 1730 until 1736, reported good weather, good visibility, no AAA fire and bombing from 4,000 feet, as debriefed:

> Two runs from west to east. Five bombs dropped in first stick, struck north center section of town and started... fires... [second] stick struck... south of road...

The 1401 crew was over Faluja from 1745 until 1750, reported unlimited visibility, no AAA fire and bombed from 3,000 feet, as debriefed:

> Two runs west to east. Incendiaries dropped in south-west of town to starboard of existing fires. Widespread areas appeared on fire, one large one and one smaller one; [second stick] slightly to starboard of first stick.

Squadron 3 pilot Walter Front flew over Gaza ahead of Squadron 106's C-46 bombers – in line with Squadron 69 recommendation and as a lesson from the prior Squadron 106 mission to bomb Gaza that had to be aborted due to poor weather – as ILAFI reported:

> Visibility was good. The purpose of the recce was meteorological observation. Flew to within a distance of approximately five miles of Gaza and then flew south of Gaza to the coast. Returned on same route and flew north of Gaza, observing clouds west of coast. The clouds were some distance from the sea. From north to Gaza to north of Majdal was followed by a searchlight. Observed large movement of our vehicles (approximately 30) on the Beer Sheba/Gaza road.

RX-131 was over Gaza from 2135 to 2202, as ILAFI reported:

> Visibility was hazy... Three runs were made... On the first run, two bombs and all the AI3 bombs were dropped between Gaza and El Arish, approximately five miles south of Gaza. On the second run, 13 bombs were dropped, probably across the old British camp situated near Dir Balah. On the third run, six bombs were dropped across the town of Dir Balah. All the bombs were seen to explode but no results were seen.

1405 was again over Faluja from 2158 until 2214, reported fair visibility and fair weather, as well as observing the bombing of Gaza and searchlight at Gaza, as debriefed:

> Two runs over target from west to east. Army searchlights cooperated well. First run, the incendiaries were dropped plus 12 three-kilogram incendiaries. A series of small fires was started between the revetments and the road. Second run, high explosives and 13 three-kilograms... were dropped...

Squadron 103 pilot Samuel Boshes flew 10 missions during HOREV - including two in C-47 1401 on the evening of 31 December 1948: the first as pilot with Adam Shatkai as captain and the second as captain with Adam Shatkai as pilot.

Squadron 103 pilot Brian Wygle tested the new Hudson 2601 on 2 January 1949; Wygle flew seven bombing missions during HOREV - six as C-47 pilot and one as C-47 captain - in addition to test flights in 1403 and 2601.

Johnny Harris (both above) was a Second World War RAF Mosquito navigator and Jules Cuburnek (in USAAF uniform) was a Second World War USAAF B-17 bombardier; together they flew 14 Squadron 69 missions during HOREV. Most of the Squadron 101, Squadron 103 and Squadron 106 air crews were Second World War veterans.

> High explosives straddled road... three hang-ups occurred in spite of double jettison attempt. All three bombs dropped in vicinity of Ramat David, two on runway upon landing and one upon approach... further use of present system dangerous to aircraft and personnel.

1401 was over Faluja from 2230 to 2240, reported very good weather, good visibility, five searchlights at Gaza, some 20mm AAA fire and bombed from 3,000 feet, as debriefed:

> Made three runs, west to east. Army did not turn [on] searchlights in spite of signal with wing lights. On the first two runs, the bombs did not drop... third run bombs hit the south-west part of town... Two lights were observed in center of [Faluja] airfield... Artillery flashes in and around Faluja. The [ILDF] Majdal searchlight was sweeping sky, illuminating aircraft on several occasions.

RX-137 was over Gaza from 2225 until 2305 and reported good visibility, as ILAFI reported:

The aircraft made four runs over target. On the first run, three bombs were dropped which fell across town. On the second run, seven bombs were dropped which started a fire in center of town. On the third run, six bombs were dropped. On the fourth run, eight bombs were dropped; on this run, five fires were observed on east side of town. Very accurate, medium ack ack and eight searchlights were encountered around town...

END OF DAY 9

USA Special Representative in Israel James McDonald arrived at Tiberias around 2300 in order to deliver the Anglo-American ultimatum to the ILPM, who wrote in his diary:

I told JM that it is true that our armed forces, while liberating our Negev, had maneuvered across the border but were already recalled... We value the friendship of USA... and there is no cause to worry that we will violate peace. Peace is our most vital interest... In private, I told JM that I wondered about the tough tone; was it necessary for a friendly power to address a small weak nation with such a tone?

DAY 10
1 JANUARY 1949

Front D Commander Yigal Alon flew to Tel Aviv, during the night of 31 December 1948 to 1 January 1949, and reported requirement for one day, but better two days, to complete the retreat from Sinai. The ILDF was ordered to finish the retreat by 0500 on 2 January.

RAID GAZA FALUJA

Time	Sqn	A/C	Crew	Mission
0135–0321	106	RX-131	Bradshaw	attack Gaza with 24*A50+AI3 bombs
0425–0555	103	1405	Katz Nathan Laron Lipman	attack Faluja with 16*A100+25*AI3 bombs
			Berger Stern Pinto	
0425–0510	1	0602	Solarsh	Dov Field Ramat David Dov Field
0607–1050	3	0114	Navot	Tel Nof Dov Field Beer Sheba Tel Nof

Squadron 101 Spitfires flew 13 sorties in six missions with 26 bombs from 31 December 1948 until 4 January 1949; the bomb rack under the right wing can be seen in this image of a Squadron 101 Spitfire taken at Hatzor during the winter of 1948 to 1949.

Squadron 103 and Squadron 106 continued to harass Gaza and Faluja from midnight until sunrise at 0638.

RX-131 was over Gaza from 0205 until 0230, as ILAFI reported:

Visibility was good... Two runs were made over target. Ten bombs were dropped across town on first run. One searchlight was extinguished by incendiaries. On second run, 14 bombs, leaflets and five boxes [of] AI3 bombs were dropped. Accurate medium ack ack was encountered.

1405 was over Faluja from 0508 until 0520, reported good visibility, good weather and no AAA fire, as debriefed:

Two runs made over target; each approximately [heading] 110. First run, eight A100 plus 10 AI3 dropped; bombs fell short of town area but in outskirts of town. Second run, eight A100 plus 15 AI3 dropped; bombs fell short of target but in town... Both bomb sticks fell in north-west outskirts of town.

ATTACK RAIL ROAD JUNCTION

Time	Sqn	A/C	Crew	Mission
0711–0802	101	2012/16	Doyle	attack with 2*70kg bombs
07:11–0755	101	2003/12	Finkel	attack with 2*70kg bombs
0720–0808	3	0405	Simantov	training

Jack Doyle and Aaron Finkel were tasked to dive-bomb the rail road junction between Rafah and El Arish. They reported unlimited visibility, as per debrief:

Flew straight to Gaza and flew along main road to Rafah. Met flak all the way down to Rafah. At Gaza, threw up heavy, abundant and very accurate flak, black puffs... lots of tracers. Finkel's plane hit in four places, three hits right behind cockpit and one big hole in rudder, also one bullet knocked out radio. Bombed road and rail junction... observed hits... on road. Also observed hits... very close to rail line. Then from El Arish headed out to sea and proceeded north along coast from two miles out on land recce; activity nil and nothing to report. At sea sighted two small sailing vessels...

SUPPORT ILNF

Time	Sqn	A/C	Crew	Mission
0750–1235	69	1602	Raisin Goldstein Harris Cuburnek	support ILNF with 16*A100 bombs
			Lichtman Kahn Goldstein Meyerson	
			Duboff Lazarus Hill	
09:10–1010	1	0412	Efrat Porat	training
0920–1010	3	0405	Zavadi	training
0940–1155	3	0407	Brown	Tel Nof Dov Field Tel Nof
1005–1217	101	2301/40	Augarten	support ILNF and patrol north-east Sinai

ILAFI Condensed Operational Summary Number 7 reported:

EGNF, flaunted by the freedom of the ILNF, came out in the open yesterday. On 31 December 1948, at 1515, two enemy warships stopped the Richard Borchard (belonging to the Atid company but British-registered)... The ship's message for help

DAY 10: 1 JANUARY 1949

Squadron 69 Crew Number 1 flew this B-17 1602 to support the ILNF on 1 January 1949. 69 Squadron Lead Navigator John Harris recalled: Just about New Year's Day we had a party and we got a message that we had to fly to intercept the ships and bomb them from medium altitude. We tried and Jules [Cuburnek] the bombardier got very close; then our fighters thought we were an Egyptian airplane so they came right behind us, but they did not shoot.

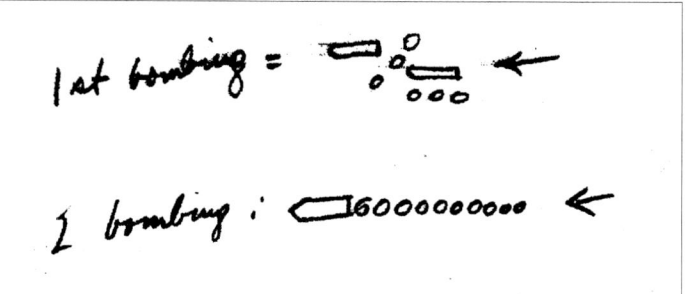

A scheme of the two bombing runs that B-17 1602 made against Egyptian warships on the morning of 1 January 1949 indicates several near misses. The naval observers remarked: Cooperation of B-17 crew excellent.

was radioed to a British warship via Cyprus. The Egyptians released the ship... On 1 January 1949 at about 0200, the same Egyptian vessels shelled... Tel Aviv... from a distance of four to five miles. About 20 shells were fired, all of which fell into sea. Three of our corvettes went out in search of Egyptian ships. At 0950 they engaged them...

Having celebrated New Year on the night of 31 December 1948 to 1 January 1949, Squadron 69 was alerted for the ILNF support mission at 0400. Take-off was set to 0600 but 1603 was not ready and the crew had to switch to 1602 which – with two ILNF observers tasked to identify ships as well as to code/decode naval messages – was over EGNF ships from 0834 until 1148.

Nine flying minutes from Hertzeliya, on briefed course, the crew saw two ships that opened fire at the bomber. Raisin climbed from 3,000 to 10,000 feet as ILNF observers tried to contact the ILNF; they were positive that the ships were not Israeli but were undecided as to the actual type of ship. Simultaneously, the crew tried to notify the ILAF at Tel Aviv but to no avail; in line with brief, the ILAF was to wire bombing orders, so the B-17 circled the ships, which changed heading and sailed west to the open sea. Meanwhile, three more ships were spotted; ILNF observers explained that these were Israeli Navy ships approaching to intercept the enemy. The crew tried to contact the ILNF ships in order to coordinate their attack but again without success. As the two naval forces engaged each other, the B-17 flew four bombing runs; dropping bombs during two runs, as Raisin reported:

> Thus the enemy fire was directed into two areas [ILAF B-17 and ILNF ships], greatly reducing his maximum concentration of firepower... As we finished our last bomb run and dropped our last bombs at an altitude of 12,000 feet, the enemy disengaged from battle and headed, like a shot out of hell, toward Port Said. Still without instruction from Tel Aviv, we continued to follow and attempted by false passes to divert his attempt. After three hours and 15 minutes over target and frantic radioing for instructions and assistance, constantly reporting back exact enemy position, we finally received word to RTB.

The B-17 departed the scene at 1148 when the EGNF ships were heading to Port Said. P-51 pilot Rudy Augarten debriefed:

> Observed two Egyptian boats being chased by three of our corvettes, the Egyptian boats were at least 50 per cent larger than our boats and quite wide. When first seen, the Egyptian boats were turning and observed shells falling in the water, but when last seen they were heading toward Port Said with our corvettes chasing them. At this time observed a B-17 flying over this engagement; it had no markings. The P-51 did not fire at him, assuming that it was our own. Then headed for coast... Found the airfield which is south of the railroad track. There were no planes on this airfield but saw one vehicle on the road to railroad station. Then observed a train approximately ten kilometers west... of about 15 cars, heading west. Then flew to Bir Hama airfield, observed one pranged, wheels-up, FIAT and one other single-engine aircraft parked near the western end of the east/west runway. Then flew to Abu Ageila and... observed a large fire and two vehicles burning near the crossroads there. Then flew to El Arish airfield and observed the same vehicle concentrations, south of long runway, as reported yesterday. Observed one Dakota in one of the pens. Then circled Bir Hama/Abu Ageila/El Arish area several times and then returned to base.

Apparently, this mission revived Squadron 69 memories from many previous ill-conceived operations - so much so that Squadron 69 Commander Al Raisin – usually not a man of words and mostly responsible for stenograph reports, if any at all – prepared, on 3 January, an exceptionally long and detailed report of that mission, which concluded with six major deficiencies from which lessons had to be drawn:

> (1) There should have been no reason why ILAF [HQ] that we were contacting should not have had the Naval Code that we were using.
> (2) Though one Mustang did arrive and stayed there for a maximum of two minutes and then vanished, it was a pity that no support should have arrived to continue the attack upon the enemy. We kept calling for Helen (P-51) and for Mickey (Spitfire) and for Ginger (B-17); none arrived. The Beaufighter would have been a tremendous help, especially with us above and the Navy on the sea diverting the attention of the enemy.
> (3) This is a second time that we have called for bombing instructions (once previously for Faluja.), that a complete lack of coordination has resulted.

(4) Though bombardier considers A100/50 is an excellent... bomb, a much heavier bomb... should have been used on this operation, and one of the near misses would surely have caused considerable damage.

(5) It is pitiful that whenever we have attempted to contact our fighters and ILNF as briefed, we cannot do this for the apparent reason that our briefed frequencies are not guarded by them.

(6) Our radio operator challenged the message that we received about RTB. He was told to standby. Then he received a message in Q Code from ILAF stating that they could not understand his message. A challenge from us to ILAF should bring out an immediate response. Our radio operator then had to resend his challenge message, and at the end of this message he added in the clear the word CHALLENGE. Then, after another five minutes' delay, our challenge was answered by the correct code and we proceeded back to base.

Possibly unknown to Raisin, the P-51 was not armed with bombs and the Beaufighter was in a sorry state, as indicated at the end of the 26 December 1948 mission.

RETREAT FROM ABU AGEILA

1047–1132	3	0405	Dankner	Tel Nof Hatzor Tel Nof
1115–1700	3	0114	Navot	Tel Nof Dov Field Tel Nof
1130–1330	1	0702	Renov	Dov Field Ramat David Haifa Dov Field
1150–1300	1	0603	Kaplan Lahat	training
1305–1650	1	0603	Kaplan	Dov Field Ramat David Dov Field
1345–1705	1	0701	Efrat Keren	Dov Field Hatzor Tel Nof Dov Field
1410–1620	2	0403		observation Gaza Strip
1412–1450	3	0106	Front	test (two flights)
1428–1557	3	0407	(Rosen)	Tel Nof Dov Field Tel Nof
1435–1447	3	0108	Giladi	test
1500–0930	3	0405	Machnes / Hirsh	test and Tel Nof Dov Field Tel Nof
1505–1605	1	0412	Renov Porat	training
1520–1650	101	2012/16	Wilson	patrol north-east Sinai
1520–1650	101	2301/40	Goodlin	patrol north-east Sinai

Squadron 101 pilots Denny Wilson and Slick Goodlin patrolled north-east Sinai during the ILDF retreat, as ILAFI reported:

> Observed no activity on Gaza/El Arish road and observed bridge on road to Abu Ageila being blown up. At Bir Hama, observed the same two aircraft as reported earlier but the tented area previously reported was no longer there. Saw no activity on the El Arish field and saw a freight train leaving El Arish station moving west. Slightly inaccurate heavy ack ack was encountered over Gaza.

Brigade 12 towed the captured Spitfire EGAF Number 664 during the retreat from Abu Ageila to Auja, but at some point during the journey one of the tires was punctured and then the undercarriage collapsed.

Following the failure of Brigade 12's tow of the captured Spitfire EGAF Number 664, an ILAF team dismantled the unfortunate fighter for subsequent transport to Tel Nof; the captured Spitfire was not repaired and never flew in ILAF service.

ATTACK GAZA FALUJA

1542–0903	3	0106	Front / Roth	Tel Nof Dov Field Hatzor Tel Nof
1550–1915	1	1301	Ospovat	Dov Field Beer Sheba Dov Field
1604–1642	3	0108	Giladi	test
1622–0945	3	0407	Ruff Roth / BarAv	Tel Nof Dov Field Tel Nof
1625–0255	106	1801	Raab Davies Bornstein Chinsky	Tel Nof as 4X-ACB Prague
1743–1830	3	0409	Biram	observation Gaza
1830–2040	1	0602	Solarsh	Dov Field Ramat David Dov Field

2037–2145	106	RX-137	Ford	
			attack Gaza with 24*50kg+AP3 bombs	
2120–2310	103	1405	Katz Nathan Laron Lipman	
			attack Faluja with 16*100kg+25*3kg bombs	
			Berger Stern Pinto	
2154–2333	103	1401	Rosin Agmon Segal Pozkanzner	
			attack Faluja with 14*A100+24*AI3 bombs	
			Erlich Greenberger	

0409 reported good weather and very good visibility over Gaza. RX-137 was over Gaza from 2115 until 2135, as ILAFI reported:

> Visibility was fair. Three runs... On the first, 10 bombs were dropped but no observations were made. On the second... eight bombs were dropped and two fires were observed, one on north edge of town and the other on the center. On the third... six bombs, five boxes of AP3 and leaflets were dropped. One big fire was observed in center of town. Very accurate medium AAA was encountered and eight or nine searchlights were seen.

1405 was over Faluja from 2200 until 2220, reported fine weather, good visibility, no AAA, and debriefed:

> First run [heading] 110; dropped four 100-kilogram bombs plus 15 three-kilogram incendiaries at intersection of lights; bombs dropping across center of town. Second run [heading] 110; dropped 12 100-kilogram bombs plus 10 three-kilogram incendiaries; same locality as first stick... On returning to base and after landing, observed object on runway which proved to be tail piece of incendiary bomb. Brought it to armorers with alibi that it had not been seen night previous. Tail piece lay on runway 24 hours before discovery and had been run over, apparently by aircraft.

1401 was over Faluja from 2233 until 2245, reported fine weather, good visibility, one burst of AAA fire and bombing from 3,800 feet, as debriefed:

> Dummy run; one small fire flickering from previous raid... Run 1 [heading] 120; eight 100-kilograms plus eight AI3s across center of town... one fire started... as approaching target... both lights switched off; released bombs in dark. Run 2 [heading] 080; six-100 kilograms plus eight AI3s; along north section of town... Run 3 [heading] 120; eight AI3s over northern part of town. Searchlights on for second two runs. Plenty of activity at Gaza. Searchlights sweeping us.

Subsequently, ILAFI reported:

> In the bombing of Faluja on the night of 1 to 2 January 1949 [there were no bombings from midnight to sunrise], when the ILDF projectors cooperated with ILAF, it is definitely known that [EGDF] HQ building was hit. The enemy suffered 10 killed and 19 wounded on this night.

DAY 11
2 JANUARY 1949

The ILDF retreated from Sinai and Front D issued a revised OPOR HOREV. The objective was still to defeat the EGDF in Israel but the new course of action was an attack against Rafah in order to cut the Gaza Strip; if the Rafah wedge succeeded, then a proposed second phase was to invade the Gaza Strip. ILDF Deputy Chief reported to the ILPM that the Rafah sector spreads over both sides of the border and that the Auja to Rafah road was mostly within Sinai, up to six kilometers deep. The ILPM figured that such a minor, tactical Israeli incursion into Sinai would not provoke British aggressiveness and approved the Front D plan.

TENSE NIGHT

0050–0250	1	0603	Ospovat	Dov Field Ramat David Dov Field
0123–0243	106	RX-131	Auerbach	
			attack Gaza with 24*50kg+AP3 bombs	

The ILAF alerted Squadron 69 for the possibility of a reprisal attack against Cairo if the EGAF or EGNF again bombed Tel Aviv, but no EGAF air raid over Israel was reported during night of 1 to 2 January 1949. The only recorded flight from Tel Nof from midnight to sunrise was RX-131, which was over Gaza from 0155 until 0159, as ILAFI reported:

> Visibility was good. Two runs... On first run, 14 bombs were dropped... direct hits... which started a few fires. On second run, 10 bombs and the AP3s were dropped... but visibility was poor, no observations were made. Light AAA was encountered.

From 0205 until 0255 a large aircraft flew over Tel Nof and Tel Aviv, at low altitude, with lights on. This was C-54 1801, which radioed a request to switch on the Tel Nof runway lights, to no avail.

The C-54 1801 ditched into the Mediterranean Sea, short of Dov Field, north of Tel Aviv, at 0255 on 2 January 1949 after Tel Nof lights were not switched on.

Due to a communication failure, the arrival of 1801 was not expected, runway lights were not turned on and the C-54 crash-landed on the coastline west of Dov Field, north of Tel Aviv.

RAID RAILWAY

0653–0800	101	2008/15	Dangott	attack railway with 2★70kg bombs
0653–0800	101	2004/14	Ruch	ditto

Squadron 101 was again tasked to dive-bomb the Egyptian railway, as ILAFI reported:

> Visibility was very good... Dive-bombed railway line at Bir Burg... but did not score any direct hits. Did not observe anything at El Arish airfield because of heavy ack ack...

ATTACK KHAN YUNES

0712–1244	3	0110	Giladi	Tel Nof Dov Field Tel Nof
0800–0915	101	0419	Goodlin	Hatzor Tel Nof Hatzor
0825–1510	1	1305	Lahat	Dov Field Beer Sheba Dov Field
0835–1225	1	1301	Kaplan	Dov Field Beer Sheba Dov Field
0838–0937	35	1106	Gibson	attack Khan Yunes with 8★100lb bombs
0838–0937	35	1102	Soltau	ditto
0838–0937	35	1105	Kaplansky	ditto
0838–0937	35	1107	Black	ditto
0845–0935	101	2018/17	Cohen	escort Flight 35
0845–0935	101	2012/16	Weizman	ditto

After two days off, Flight 35 was back in action with TOT over Khan Yunes from 0910 until 0911, as ILAFI reported:

> Visibility was good. All bombs were dropped and were seen exploding on and around target area (police station in center of town)...

Escorts reported unlimited visibility, as ILAFI indicated:

> Observed bombs falling in courtyard of police station and others on buildings south of police station.

ATTACK EL ARISH

0850–1050	69	1601	Feldman Ratushniak Jacobs Weissbrod	attack El Arish with 16★A100 bombs Fink Soltan Nash Lowenberg Lazarus Gershaw
0855–1048	69	1602	McConville Spink Seftel Weinstein	attack El Arish with 16★100kg bombs Cohen Schwartzbach Christiensen Kaplan Robinson Liponetzky Cohen Joffe
0857–1048	69	1603	Noach Maseng Bresslof Michel	attack El Arish with 16★100kg bombs Swiel Majzels Wadman Spicehandler Jacobson
0920–1030	101	2002/11	Wilson	escort Squadron 69
0920–1030	101	2004/14	Goodlin	ditto

Squadron 69 pilot Sam Feldman (center) and Squadron 103 radio operators Phil Kemp (left) and Milton Boettger (right) were photographed at Ramat David on 1 January 1949 as they greeted the New Year in good spirits.

The B-17s were over El Arish marshaling yards from 1000 to 1002. Crews reported fair to good weather, good to excellent visibility, inaccurate AAA and bombing from 13,500 feet, but all missed the target, as 1601 debriefed:

> One run [heading] 030. Missed target, hit sea. Drop started 100 yards from coast, did not reach land at all. Pilot suggests [in order to hit target] bombing height of 1,000 feet [because] flak... inaccurate.

The escorts' observation was similar, as ILAFI reported:

> Visibility was excellent. Escorted B-17s to El Arish marshaling yards and observed all bombs fall in the sea... Slight... inaccurate AAA... from El Arish.

TROOP TRAIN

0930–1200	1	0603	Renov	Dov Field Ramat David Haifa Dov Field
0933–1035	1	0702	Lavi	training
0945–1000	1	0412	Porat	training
0953–1200	3	0114	Roth	Tel Nof Dov Field Tel Nof
1012–1117	3	0407	BarAv	training
1020–1127	101	0419	Ruch	Hatzor Tel Nof Hatzor
1023–1050		2601	Wygle	test new Hudson at Tel Nof
1045–1052	1	0412	Kraft	training
11–32–1216	101	0419		Hatzor Tel Nof Hatzor
1141–		2601	Wygle	Tel Nof Dov Field
1149–1158	3	0108	Moller	test
1210–1314	101	2002/11	Feldman	attack railway
1210–1314	101	2013/18	Finkel	ditto

Squadron 101 was again tasked to cut the railroad west of El Arish. Pilots reported unlimited visibility, no AAA and bombing from 5,000 to 1,000 feet, as debriefed:

> Dive-bombed track but one pair of bombs failed to explode and the other bombs missed the track. At this, observed a train

with approximately eight cars... In all, five passes were made at the engine and four passes at the cars. Numerous strikes... on the engine and cars and as the train halted, at least 30 soldiers were seen jumping from train and running into sands. In all probability this was a troop train.

MARSHALING YARDS

Time	Sqn	A/C	Pilot(s)	Mission
1240–1400	1	0602	Ospovat	Dov Field Hatzor Dov Field
125317023		0110	Giladi	Tel Nof Beer Sheba Dov Field Tel Nof
1337–1344	101	2019/19		Tel Nof Hatzor delivery to Squadron 101
1432–1533	3	0407	Simantov	Tel Nof Dov Field Tel Nof
1451–1624	3	0108	Brown	observation Judea
1455–1655	69	1603	Noach Maseng Jacobs Michel Kahn Majzels Swiel Spicehandler Jacobson	attack railway with 16*100kg bombs
1457–1650	69	1601	Feldman Ratushniak Bresslof Weissbrod Soltan Lowenberg Fink Lazarus Nash Wadman	attack railway with 16*100kg bombs
1457–1650	69	1602	McConville Spink Seftel Weinstein Christiensen Cohen Robinson Kaplan Cohen Liponetzky Kapusa	attack railway with 16*100kg bombs
1526–1552	101	2012/16	Sinclair	escort Squadron 69
1526–1617	101	2018/17	McElroy	ditto

Squadron 69 repeated its morning mission to the El Arish marshaling yards. The trio flew one bombing run, from 1605, at 12,500 feet. The trail of bombs fell roughly 60 degrees to the railway line, with some of the bombs falling on the railway line. The B-17s actually attacked without an escort, as ILAFI reported:

> Visibility was fair. One [Squadron 101] aircraft, owing to engine trouble, RTB. The second aircraft... Proceeded to El Arish... and after circling area and not seeing the B-17s, RTB.

B-17 1601 was the lead ship during most of the Squadron 69 missions from July 1948 until January 1949. Possibly for this reason Sam Feldman, who previously flew most of his missions in 1602, switched to 1601 when flying as Hammers leader on 2 January 1949. The lead bomber arrived in Israel with two Direction Finding (DF) loop antennas in streamlined casings right behind a sword antenna that towered above the cockpit, but after arrival the forward DF antenna was removed; also visible are the external bomb racks under the wings.

Obviously, it may have been chance that the unescorted B-17s did not meet enemy aircraft, but the fact was that enemy aircraft had not been reported over north-east Sinai since 31 December 1949, while Noach concluded his report with a gladdening observation:

> El Arish airfield seemed completely deserted.

ATTACK FALUJA

Time	Sqn	A/C	Pilot(s)	Mission
1526–1647	3	0409	Zavadi	Tel Nof Dov Field Tel Nof
15 30–1630	1	0412	Efrat Porat	training
1600–1631	3	0106	Roth	Tel Nof Dov Field
1626–1631	101	Spitfire	Wilson	Tel Nof Tel Nof (test)
1637–1700	106	RX-133	Lewis	test
1640–1650	1	1301	Renov	test
1706–1729	3	0407	Moller	Tel Nof Dov Field
1738–1908	103	1405	Boshes Wygle Kenny Manor	attack Faluja with 16*A100 bombs
1755–1900	1	0602	Solarsh	Dov Field Ramat David Dov Field
1757–1900	3	0409	Hirsh	observation weather Gaza
1814–1952	103	1406	Shatkai Keidar Adler Kemp Berger Hollander Pinto	attack Faluja with 16A100kg+25*AI3 bombs

1405 was over Faluja from 1824 until 1833, reported good weather, good visibility, no AAA and bombing from 3,000 feet in two runs, dropping eight bombs in each, and concluding its debrief with a positive impression:

> Excellent cooperation with army on searchlights. Vertical beam out Julis not on but also not needed.

1406 was over Faluja from 1859 until 1906, reported good weather, good visibility, no AAA and bombing from 3,200 feet in two runs, as debriefed:

The Egyptian newspaper *El Aharam* published this photo on 2 January 1949 with the misleading caption: Part of an Israeli aircraft brought down by Egyptian forces in southern Palestine; which was correct except for the fact that ILAF Squadron 101 S199 D-110 was lost over the Gaza Strip in July 1948. No ILAF fighters were lost in combat during HOREV.

Flight 35 T-6 1105 was damaged during an enemy raid on the evening of 2 January 1949; it was repaired and returned to fly by 5 January 1949.

> Run 1 direction 110; eight A100 plus 19 AI3... dropped in line across center of town. Run 2 direction 150; eight A100... plus six AI3... dropped; this stick also fell across center of town... Our searchlight beacons intersected approximately at town center and bombs hit there...

ATTACK FALUJA/GAZA

2125–2250	103	1405	Wygle Boshes Kenny Manor attack Faluja with 16*A100kg bombs
2135–2252	106	RX-131	Levett attack Gaza with 24*A50+AI3 bombs
2225–2330	106	RX-137	Breier attack Gaza with 24*A50+AI3 bombs
2314–0047	103	1406	Shatkai Keidar Adler Kemp attack Faluja with 16*A100+25*AI3 bombs Pinto Hollander Berger
23:58-00:55	106	RX-133	Levett attack Gaza with 24*A50+AI3 bombs

Enemy aircraft – possibly EGAF Stirlings – bombed Jerusalem from 1940 and Tel Nof from 2000; approximately 14 bombs were dropped over Jerusalem and four people were injured; some 10 incendiary bombs were dropped over Tel Nof and Flight 35 1105 was damaged.

The ILAF bombing campaign continued with 1405, which was over Faluja from 2210 to 2215, reported very good weather, good visibility, no AAA, bombing from 3,000 feet and two runs, each heading 120, with eight bombs dropped in each run. RX-131 was over Gaza from 2216 to 2226, as ILAFI reported:

> Visibility was fair. Three runs... On first run, 10 bombs were dropped and observed to fall in center of target area. On second run, eight bombs were dropped and explosions were seen on southern edge of target. On third run, six bombs and five boxes of AI3s were dropped and were observed exploding in center of target area. One burst of... light and inaccurate ack ack was encountered. No lights were observed.

RX-137 followed from 2255 until 2305, as ILAFI reported:

> Visibility was good. Two runs... First run 14 bombs... dropped and... seen exploding in the northern edge of town. Second run, 10 bombs and five boxes of AI3s were dropped and were observed falling across town. Large fires were seen burning on east side of target. No ack ack and no searchlights were seen over target area.

1406 was over Faluja from 2359 until 0006 and bombed from 3,500 feet, as debriefed:

> Run 1 [heading] 130; eight A100... and 20 incendiaries dropped... in area between airfield perimeter and Manshiya road... Run 2 [heading] 125; eight A100... and eight incendiaries dropped... Searchlights were beamed only in interval between runs, possibly due to late arrival over target.

RX-133 was over Gaza from 0013 until 0024, as ILAFI reported:

> Visibility was good. Two runs... Run 1; 16 bombs... dropped; all exploded in center of town. Run 2; eight bombs and... five boxes of AI3s... dropped... No searchlights and no ack ack...

DAY 12
3 JANUARY 1949

Front D operations, in line with the revised OPOR HOREV, were set to start after sunset on 3 January with an attack aimed to occupy Rafah barracks, thus disconnecting the Gaza Strip from Sinai.

HARASS FALUJA/GAZA

0110–0240	103	1405	Boshes Wygle Kenny Manor attack Faluja with 16*A100 bombs
0115–0220	106	RX-137	Breier attack Gaza with 24*A50+AI3 bombs

Squadron 103 and Squadron 106 continued to harass Faluja and Gaza. 1405 was over Faluja from 0157 until 0203, reported fair weather, good visibility, no AAA over Faluja but six searchlights and heavy AAA fire over Gaza, and bombed from 3,000 feet:

> Two runs, both at [heading] 120, eight bombs dropped each run... [ILDF] searchlights came on after first run.

RX-137 was over Gaza, reported good visibility there and flew two runs, as ILAFI indicated:

> On first run, three bombs were dropped which were observed falling on northern side of town. On second run, 21 bombs and five boxes of AI3s were dropped and were observed falling across center of town. One large fire was observed burning on west side of target. Six searchlights were in operation, obviously radar-controlled, which caught the aircraft immediately, when it was on its second run. Intense accurate 75mm ack ack was encountered and it is thought, by crew, that guns of a heavier caliber than previously reported were being used.

RAID KHAN YUNES

0634–	101	2008/15)	Senior	patrol Faluja Pocket Gaza Strip
0634–	101	2018/17)	Peake	ditto
0730–0755	3	0110	Brown	Tel Nof Dov Field
0830–1955	1	1305	Efrat	Dov Field Haifa St Jean Ramat David Dov Field
0830–0942	35	1102	Flint	attack Khan Yunes with 8*50kg bombs

DAY 12: 3 JANUARY 1949

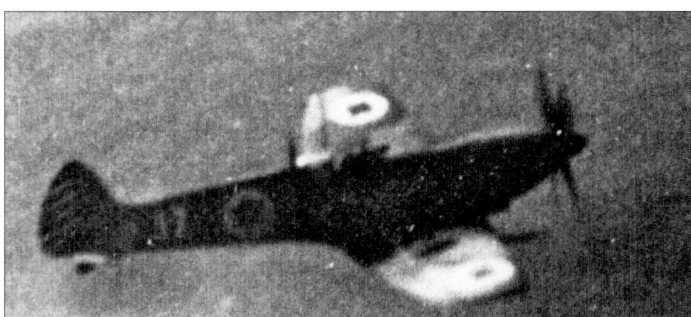

Squadron 101 pilots Boris Senior and Waine Peake flew Spitfires 2008/15 and 2018/17 during the early morning hours on 3 January 1949.

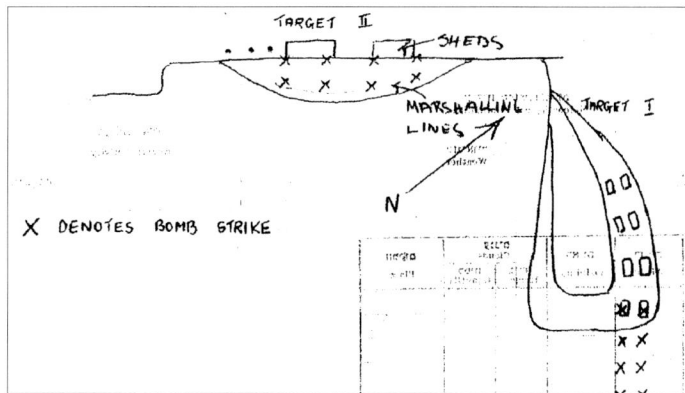

A Squadron 101 debrief sketch of Squadron 69 bombing Rafah on 3 January 1949.

> 100 vehicles parked in a very congested, disorderly manner... the concentration consisted of mainly trucks, at least four half-tracks and no ambulances. A fair amount of medium flak was encountered from Khan Yunes.

RAID RAFAH

0831–0943	35	1106	Gibson	ditto
0832–0944	35	1107	Dougherty	ditto
0840–1004	101	2003/11	McElroy	escort Flight 35
0840–1004	101	2004/14	Sinclair	ditto

In preparation for the start of the renewed HOREV attack in the Gaza Strip sector, the ILAF raided targets in the Gaza Strip, with Flight 35 attacking Khan Yunes from 0910 until 0911, as ILAFI reported:

> Visibility was good. Two runs... One bomb was hang-up. Target... (consisting of eight small tents) was definitely hit. On second run, bombs were dropped along railway; no direct hits were observed. 20mm AAA was encountered.

Escorts may have rendezvoused with bombers after the first run and after the attack patrolled north-east Sinai, to monitor EGDF redeployment in sectors from which the ILDF retreated, as ILAFI reported:

> Visibility was excellent. Observed Harvards bombing the road to the north of Khan Yunes town just in front of railway junction. All six bombs exploded, first two south of road and the other four were possibly near misses or on road. Recce Rafah/Auja road... only two vehicles on road... proceeding towards Auja. At Auja crossroads two stationary cars. On Auja/Abu Ageila road observed two trucks... a stationary car and a truck moving towards Auja... four stationary vehicles... at Abu Ageila crossroads two parked trucks; three light trucks led by a Jeep on Abu Ageila/Bir/Hama road... proceeding towards Abu Ageila; 30 vehicles, including many open trucks carrying troops, and also many Jeeps, on main road from Abu Ageila to El Arish... these vehicles were in convoy formation and there appeared to be no armor in the convoy; on the approach of the aircraft the convoy stopped and the men ran for cover. On Abu Ageila/El Arish road, to the west of road, in parking area...

0900–1055	69	1601	Raisin Ben Porat Harris Cuburnek	attack Rafah with 16*100kg bombs
			Lichtman Goldstein Aronson	
			Meyerson Duboff Gershaw	
			Gershenson	
0901–1050	69	1602	Feldman Ratushniak	ditto
			Bresslof	
			Weissbrod Fink Soltan Lowenberg	
			Lazarus Nash Wadman	
0923–1048	101	2002/11	Feldman	escort Squadron 69
0923–1048	101	2013/18	Finkel	ditto

The B-17s flew two runs over Rafah railway station; the first from 0952 until 0956 at 15,500 feet and the second from 1003 until 1007 at 16,500 feet. The weather was good and AAA was heavy and accurate.

During the first run, the lead aircraft dropped six bombs and the wingman dropped eight bombs. Feldman's crew reported:

> A building was hit and blew-up with great impact, and then black smoke came high up. By the blast presumed to be ammo dump.

The second run was aimed at the marshaling yards; Raisin's crew reported:

> Bombs overshot marshaling yard. Burst started at north edge of yards and landed amongst four buildings and in tented area. Arming wires are of insufficient strength and improperly rigged.

The second B-17 also missed the marshaling yards, so:

> Crew recommends hitting target again as well as Khan Yunes. Both places packed with "goods"!

Escorts reported visibility as slightly hazy and AAA as medium, inaccurate but intense:

> Picked up the two B-17s at rendezvous, proceeding inland south avoiding Gaza [Faluja?] Pocket and came in over Rafah

from near Gvulot. Proceeded directly to target, an initial run, they both went in for target 1 and observed eight strikes. Then Forts went out to sea, made a wide inland sweep and made run 2 from same direction as run 1. Observed eight strikes on target 2. Escorted Forts to about five miles north of Tel Aviv.

Target 1 hit two end sheds; burned out quickly... smoke continued to a height of about 1,000 feet, very dark gray smoke. Target 2 straddled... among rails and sheds of marshaling yards; bombing of this target very effective.

CAMEL CARAVANS

0946–1432	3	0405	Lee	Tel Nof Haifa Tel Nof
1044–1153	1	0412	Kraft	training
1054–1555	35	Bet55/0804	Soltau	TelN of St Jean Tel Nof
1102–1151	3	0407	Simantov	training
1130–1450	1	1301	Solarsh	Dov Field Beer Sheba Dov Field
1140–1548	1	0602	Renov	Dov Field Ramat David Dov Field
1200–1220	3	0106	Ruff	Tel Nof Ramat David
1209–1346	3	0409	Navot	observation Judea
1210–1237	3	0407	Simantov	Tel Nof Hatzor Tel Nof
1211–1331	101	0419	Cohen	Hatzor Tel Nof Hatzor

Squadron 3 pilot Nathan Navot was tasked to monitor activity east of the Faluja Pocket and pinpointed three camel caravans.

RAID KHAN YUNES

1252–1350	35	1102	Flint	attack Khan Yunes with 8*50kg bombs
1253–1351	35	1106	Gibson	ditto
1254–1352	35	1107	Dougherty	ditto
1300–1404	101	2004/14	Jacobs	escort Flight 35
1300–1404	101	2008/15	Peake	ditto

Flight 35 was again over Khan Yunes from 1320 until 1321, as ILAFI reported:

> Visibility was good. One run... All bombs exploded across Khan Yunes/Gaza road. Traffic on road was then strafed. Medium accurate AAA fire was encountered.

The escorts also attacked, as ILAFI reported:

> Visibility was good but slightly hazy. Did not observe where bombs fell but saw smoke rising above road in north of Khan Yunes. After escorting Harvards portion of the way back, returned to Gaza/El Arish road. Strafed vehicles... Observed strikes on three trucks, three cars and one armored car. The trucks contained soldiers. The trucks were left burning. Slight, light, fairly accurate AAA...

RAID ABU AGEILA

1332–1500	101	2003/12)	Dangott	attack El Arish with 2*70kg bombs

Flight 35 pilot Chester Black tested BT-13 1001 - photographed inside a hangar at Tel Nof - on 3 January 1949; the trainer - used as a hack - is not known to have flown since 5 December 1948, when Squadron 101 pilot Jack Doyle flew the BT-13 from Hatzor to Tel Nof for AMU maintenance.

1332–1500	101	2002/11)	Ruch	ditto
1400–1610	1	0701	Ospovat	Dov Field Beer Sheba Dov Field
1401–1455	3	0114	Roth	observation Faluja
1421–1457	3	0407	Bar Av	training
1427–1510	101	0419	Levett	Hatzor Tel Nof Hatzor
1430–1450		1001	Black	test
1440–1453	101	2017/20	Wilson	Tel Nof Hatzor delivery to Squadron 101

Squadron 101 dive-bombed, as ILAFI reported:

> Visibility was good. Did not observe reported large concentration of vehicles south of El Arish [since by then EGDF redeployed following ILDF retreat] but saw 30 vehicles on El Arish/AbuAgeila road... bombed four stationary armored vehicles at Abu Ageila crossroads; at least one hit was observed. Strafing passes were also made on eight or nine vehicles which were in the above [-mentioned] convoy. Men were seen jumping from vehicles, some of which were turned off road into sand.

Squadron 3 Auster 0114 was tasked to monitor activity west of the Faluja Pocket but nothing unusual was observed.

REVISIT RAFAH

1500–1650	69	1601	Raisin Goldstein Harris Cuburnek	attack Rafah with 16*100kg bombs Lichtman Goldstein Aronson Meyerson Duboff Gershaw Gershenson
1500–1650	69	B-17	Noach Maseng Jacobs Michel Kellman Swiel Kahn Spicehandler Jacobson Hill	ditto
1520–1609	3	0405	Katzin	training
1520–1620	1	0412	Porat	training
1527–1640	101	2018/15)	Cohen	escort Squadron 69
1530–1630	35	1001	Black	training

Possibly, escort leader Syd Cohen had to switch from Spitfire to P-51 and took off eight minutes after escort wingman Jack Cohen, as ILAFI reported:

> Visibility was poor. Observed bombs falling near large stores buildings in western part of Rafah camp area. After escorting B-17 to Majdal, did a shipping recce to area between Gaza and El Arish but observed no shipping. The P-51 then flew over El Arish/Abu Ageila road and... Abu Ageila/Auja road... encountered light and medium AAA [over Abu Ageila/Auja road] and heavy inaccurate AAA from Rafah.

RAID DIR BALAH

1545–1632	35	1102	Flint	attack Dir Balah with 8*50kg bombs
1546–1633	35	1106	Gibson	ditto
1547–1634	35	1107	Dougherty	ditto
1556–1654	101	2004/14	Levett	escort Flight 35
1556–1654	101	2008/15	Wilson	ditto

Flight 35 was over Dir Balah from 1622 to 1623, as ILAFI reported:

> Visibility was hazy. Each aircraft made one run along railway line to north-east and all bombs fell in target area. A large amount [of] 20mm very accurate AAA fire and a few rounds of 40mm AAA fire were encountered.

The escorts observed bombs hit both sides of the railway south of Dir Balah and reported AAA as slight, light and inaccurate.

The B-17s were escorted on most of the daytime bombing missions but were never intercepted by Egyptian fighters. Squadron 101 pilot Jack Cohen escorted Squadron 69 to Rafah, on 3 January 1949, in Spitfire 2018/17 - photographed from the B-17 waist gun position during fighter affiliation training on 25 April 1949 - while Syd Cohen flew P-51 2302.

1533–0945	3	0409	Hirsh	Tel Nof Dov Field Tel Nof
1535–17:00	101	2013/2302	Cohen	escort Squadron 69

Squadron 69 revisited Rafah from 1558 until 1603 but this time bombed the barracks. Crews reported the weather as hazy and bombed from 16,500 feet in the face of inaccurate medium and heavy AAA. The lead bombardier reported:

> This was a typical "Cuburnek maneuver". There was much haze over target – after two minutes' search, with capable support from navigator [John Harris] we identified target. I dropped one side of bomb bay. Noticing that I was a fraction of an inch left of center of target, I gave the pilot a fast one degree right and then dropped the rest of the load. This split-second decision made the difference between a good hit and an excellent one – which it was. Nearly all the bombs hit various buildings in target area.

All bombs were released during a single run and fell in the target area, according to the lead crew, or were 'bull' on target area as reported by the wingman crew. Three single-engine aircraft heading south were observed west of Gaza at 1609 and the bomber crews concluded that the fighter escort went to intercept them, but this was not the case and these aircraft were probably Flight 35 T-6s on the way to Dir Balah. Raisin's crew also remarked:

> Crew reports one of escorting fighters did not have its nose painted red (Mustang). It would be advisable to use uniform nose color for our fighters to avoid misunderstandings.

The first two ILAF Spitfires had elliptical wing tips while subsequent VELVETTA and VELVETTA 2 Spitfires had clipped wing tips; the VELVETTA Spitfires - which arrived in Israel during September 1948 - had the Squadron 101 badge painted on the left engine cowling by the time of HOREV.

The VELVETTA 2 Spitfires arrived during HOREV and were rushed into combat so there was no time, nor attention, to paint the Squadron 101 badge on the left engine cowling.

HARASS FALUJA

Time	Sqn	A/C	Crew	Route/Notes
1627–1645	3	0110	Roth	Dov Field Tel Nof
1642–1701	3	0106	Front	training
1646–1708	3	0407	Machnes	Tel Nof Dov Field
1713–1843	103	1405	Orringer Agmon Festing Aronson Hollander Greenberger Stern	attack Faluja with 16*A100+25*AI3 bombs
1740–2110	1	1301	Kaplan	Dov Field Beer Sheba Dov Field
1744–1923	103	1406	Katz Nathan Weinstein Boettger Erlich Berger Pinto	attack Faluja with 16*A100+25*AI3 bombs
1747–1900	3	0405	Roth	(observation weather Gaza)
2024–2225	103	1405	Orringer Agmon Festing Aronson Hollander Greenberger Stern	attack Faluja with 16*A100+30*AI3 bombs
2052–2130	103	1406	Katz Nathan Weinstein Boettger Erlich Berger Pinto	attack Faluja with 16*A100+25*AI3 bombs
2132–2255	3	0405	Moller	observation weather Gaza
2344–0118	103	1405	Orringer Agmon Festing Aronson Hollander Stern	attack Faluja with 16*A100+30*AI3 bombs

The ILDF initiated an attack against Rafah and the ILAF refrained from bombing the Gaza Strip so only the Faluja Pocket was harassed during the night of 3 to 4 January.

1405 was over Faluja from 1751 until 1755, reported good visibility and bombed from 3,000 feet in two runs.

1406 was over Faluja from 1820 to 1837, reported fair weather, good visibility and bombed from 3,500 feet in two runs.

1405 was again over Faluja from 2128 until 2148, reported good weather and bombed from 3,000 feet in three runs.

1406 did not attack during the second sortie, as debriefed:

> Took off normal power. Circled field once. Headed 235 and continued to climb. At approximately 10 minutes after take-off, saw port engine burning through cowl flaps, evidently completely around engine. Cut all switches... to port engine and turned fire extinguisher on... Fire continued to burn two minutes after all switches off. Decided to jettison over sea, continued direct course to sea and dropped stick at about 10-second interval, started dropping almost quarter mile out to sea. Turned back in and started dropping incendiaries, all except two fell into sea. The remaining two fell on dunes, one went off... Came back on one engine. Tower cooperation excellent! Came in too high first approach, had to go around.

The ILAF did not bomb the Gaza Strip but Squadron 3 flew the evening weather reconnaissance mission, flying over the area from 2212 until 2220, as ILAFI reported:

> Observed 6/10 cloud moving in from sea over Gaza where visibility was hazy. The searchlights at Gaza were observed sweeping the ground and tracers seemed to have been fired from east side of Gaza, possibly ground action.

1405 returned to Faluja from 0028 until 0041, reported good weather, bombed from 3,500 feet in three runs and, upon RTB, inspected blackout:

> Tel Aviv blackout improving but can still [be] improved. Rest of Israel well lit...

DAY 13
4 JANUARY 1949

Front D's pincer attack against Rafah was launched during the night of 3 to 4 January. Brigade 1 attacked east of Rafah; Brigade 12 advanced to west of Rafah along road from Auja; Brigade 8 and Brigade 10 were in reserve. The ILAF did not raid the Gaza Strip during night of 3 to 4 January, thus avoiding any potential for 'friendly fire' incidents.

RAID RAILWAY

Time	Sqn	A/C	Crew	Notes
0600–	2	0402		observation Gaza Strip
0655–0815	101	2003/12	Cohen	attack rail with 2*70kg bombs
0655–0815	101	2013/18	Cohen	ditto
0700–	2	0408		observation Gaza Strip

0402 was tasked to monitor activity around Rafah but mostly reported air activity:

> At... observed... fighters... coming from south at approx. 1,600 feet; two other fighters followed them; they circled the camp [along Imara to Rafah road] and bombed locality. Above Imara saw two aircraft proceeding south along coast towards Rafah; they were fired on by AAA; subsequently saw them return; they were our aircraft. At 0700, approximately, observed a Dakota proceeding south from coast; on a course south of Imara.

The fighters were possibly EGAF. The two friendly fighters flying return to Rafah were probably Syd Cohen and Jack Cohen:

> Visibility was good... Dive-bombed train near Khan Yunes. One pair of bombs missed and the other fell between railway line and an encampment of approximately 36 tents... Thereafter... strafed train – which consisted of about 10 cars – and strikes were observed on engine which gave off steam. Later, 20 stationary vehicles... were observed. Approximately 12 stationary railway trucks... were also strafed but results were not seen. Returned to scene of first attack on train, which was seen to have remained stationary... flak was encountered from Rafah area and from train area. Flak was also encountered over stationary railway trucks, light and medium, and accurate.

From 0730 until 0815, 0408 ranged artillery that bombarded Khan Yunes.

DAY 13: 4 JANUARY 1949

Squadron 69 servicemen at Ramat David, from left to right: Hans Weissbrod (navigator ex-RAF), Johnny Harris (navigator ex-RAF), Lem Kaplan (gunner ex-USAAF), Jorgen Christienson (gunner from Denmark), Paul, Zan Swartzberg (gunner from South Africa) and Max Cohen (engineer ex-USAAF).

Squadron 101 pilots Caesar Dangott (left) and Rudy Augarten (right) at Hatzor in March 1949; Dangott flew VELVETTA 2 Spitfire 2008 from Yugoslavia to Israel on 23 December 1948 and then flew nine HOREV missions.

RAID GAZA

0727–1722	3	0110	Roth	Tel Nof Dov Field Tel Nof
0840–1445	1	1305	Solarsh	Dov Field Beer Sheba Dov Field
0840–1200	1	1301	Kaplan	Dov Field Beer Sheba Dov Field
0845–1050	1	0701	Renov	Dov Field Ramat David Dov Field
0913–1038	69	1601	Feldman Ratushniak Bresslof attack Gaza with 40★A50 bombs Weissbrod Soltan Dinkin Fink Nash Lazarus Wadman Kapusa	
0914–1036	69	1603	McConville Spink Seftel Cohen attack Gaza with 32★50kg bombs Christiensen Schwartzbach Robinson Kaplan Cohen Liponetzky	
0930–1113	101	2004/14	Dangott	escort Squadron 69
0930–1113	101	2008/15	Jacobs	ditto

Squadron 69 was over Gaza from 0955 until 0957; crews reported good weather, good visibility and bombed in single run – headings 331 and 350 – from 12,000 feet in face of AAA fire that was described as wide and inaccurate. The escorts reported:

> Visibility was unlimited. Carried out escort duty and observed bombs bursting in southern part of Gaza but saw no actual hits. After escorting B-17s back, recced El Arish/Abu Ageila road area. Strafed three trucks... observed strikes and cars halted. Recced part of Abu Ageila/Bir Hama road; saw no transport; observed three armored cars... on road; strafed one of them and observed strikes. Heavy, inaccurate AAA from Gaza.

RAID RAFAH

1000–1028	35	1001	Dougherty	training
1010–1105	3	0405	Front	observation Front B
1013–1035	3	0407	Giladi	Dov Field Tel Nof
1023–1053	101	0419	Cohen	Hatzor Tel Nof Hatzor
1024–1705	35	Bet55 /0804	Gibson	Tel Nof Dov Field Tel Nof
1030–1038	35	1001	Woolfe	training
1045–1105	1	1302	Lahat	test
1050–1145	35	1102	Flint	attack Rafah with 8★50kg bombs
1050–1145	35	1106	Kaplansky	ditto
1050–1145	35	1107	Brown	ditto
1055–1110	3	0407	Navot	training
1055–1115	35	1001	Baker	training
1100–1225	101	2013/18	Wilson	escort Flight 35 and attack with 2★70kg bombs
1100–1225	101	2002/11	Ruch	ditto

At 1100, OWL HQ reported:

> Our Spitfires attacked, this morning, an enemy train transporting troops; the train was damaged and stopped between Rafah and Khan Yunes; send Harvards and Spitfires [to attack train].

Flight 35 was tasked to attack the train near Rafah and was over the target from 1125 until 1126:

> The runs were made south [to] north along track. Four bombs fell slightly to left of engine and four near end of train slightly to west. Although it was seen to move afterwards, damage is believed to have been caused. One aircraft dropped four bombs in a gun position south of target, one gun is thought to have been hit directly. Heavy accurate AAA fire was encountered from 40mm and 75mm or 88mm guns.

The Squadron 101 pair escorted and then attacked:

> Escorted Harvards to area between Khan Yunes and Rafah where train previously seen... train was moving south-west; observed Harvards to bomb and straddle train. Escorted Harvards back and returned when train had already pulled into Rafah station. Observed three stationary trucks 10 kilometers north of Abu Ageila; these were dive-bombed, results

unknown. Thereafter strafed trucks and observed hits. Intense accurate AAA fire from Rafah; one aircraft was hit.

Subsequent feedback from the ILDF indicated that this Flight 35 mission was, unintentionally, the only significantly successful ILAF close air support mission during HOREV:

On 4 January 1949, three of our Harvards dive-bombed the Rafah area at about 1130. On the first run of our planes, bombs fell in front of counter-attacking enemy forces, greatly demoralizing them. In the other two runs, the bombs fell well within the camp area.

SCRAMBLES

1120–1225	3	0407	Giladi	scramble
1127–1222	101	2003/12)	Cohen	scramble
1127–1222	101	2301/40	Schroeder	scramble

A reported bombardment of the Gedera sector prompted the scramble of 0407 to seek enemy ships, but none were noted, while the Squadron 101 pair followed:

Scramble after reported enemy aircraft but none was seen. Thereafter flew to Auja, El Arish and Bir Hama; the condition of the latter is unchanged.

CASEVAC

	1	1301	Ospovat	Dov Field Beer Sheba Auja Dov Field
1205–1515	1	0701	Efrat	Dov Field Ramat David Tel Nof Dov Field
1207–1615	3	0405	Katzin Biram	Tel Nof Ramat David Dov Field Tel Nof
1253–1853	106	RX-136	Applebaum	VELVETTA 2 Niksic Tel Nof
1355–1735	1	0412	Hofshi	Dov Field Beer Sheba Dov Field
1505–1531	3	0407	Zavadi	Tel Nof Hatzor Tel Nof
1506–1750	3	0114	Ruff	Tel Nof Ramat David Tel Nof

Squadron 1's Rapide 1301 and the two Norecrins were capable of flying missions as ambulances; Squadron 2 Commander Arie Rubens may have been unaware that 1301 was also an ambulance, as implied from his 4 January report:

At 0230 we were notified of a severely wounded [soldier] at Auja who must be transported to Tel Aviv... We requested an ambulance aircraft and dispatched a Piper... to Auja in order to mark strip [for ambulance aircraft]... The requested Norecrin did not arrive... Leon Ospovat [who arrived at Beer Sheba in 1301] agreed to try... Landed successfully [at Auja] and transported wounded directly to Tel Aviv.

LANDING ACCIDENT

1510–1645	101	2013/12	Senior	patrol Gaza Strip

Squadron 1 Rapide 1301 was inaugurated as an ambulance - and photographed - on 16 November 1948; in this Rapide Squadron 1, pilot Leon Ospovat evacuated a casualty from Auja to Tel Aviv on 4 January 1949.

Squadron 101 pilot Aaron Finkel standing beside Spitfire 2004/14 after a landing accident on 4 January 1949.

The extent of damage to Spitfire 2004/14 following the landing accident on 4 January 1949 is evident in this view; 2004 never flew again.

1510–1645	101	2004/14	Finkel	ditto

Squadron 101 did not maintain continuous cover over the battlefield during daylight, but, from time to time, patrols flew over the Gaza Strip:

Patrolled Gaza to Rafah, Rafah to Gaza along main road; made four to five circuits. Eight to 10 small vehicles scattered on main Gaza/Rafah road, traveling in both directions. More activity closer to Gaza/Dir Balah sector. Then followed main Rafah/Auja road; saw 60 to 85 vehicles traveling towards Auja; some were parked on sides of road; also some armor; some moving in convoy formation about 50 yards apart... then a distinct break and nothing for about five kilometers southwards; then small concentration of people where main road crossed Egyptian border. Observed Forts bombing in northern part, near some sheds... On landing, Finkel paid out too high and flipped over.

RAID RAFAH

1525–1702	69	1601	Feldman Ratushniak Bresslof attack Rafah with 39★A50 bombs Weissbrod Dinkin Fink Nash Lazarus Jackson
1526–1707	69	1603	McConville Spink Seftel Weinstein attack Rafah with 40★50frag bombs Cohen Christiensen Schwartzbach Robinson Kaplan Cohen Gershenson
1530–1542	103	1403	Shatkai test Tel Nof Tel Nof
1545–1658	101	2012/16	Feldman escort Squadron 69
1545–1658	101	2008/15	Sinclair ditto

The B-17s flew a single run – from south to north, headings 340 and 345 – at 16,000 feet from 1619 to 1620. AAA over Rafah was reported as heavy (type) and accurate (fire). Six of 1601's bombs fell late, including two that fell on land and four into the sea. McConville's crew concluded:

> Stick fell in the west part of target 3 and along to target 1... Target 2 was entirely missed due to faulty approach. Crew not very happy about the result.

Bombers and escorts did not rendezvous:

> Orbited rendezvous [point] 30 minutes then ordered... to proceed to target area. Did so, patrolled target area for 15 minutes. Then ordered to RTB. At Rafah, noticed long gray line of smoke blowing inland. Did not see Forts at all; Forts must have arrived ahead of [planned rendezvous time] and did not wait for fighter escort. [During flight heard] on radio JACK 1 [who] talked in Arabic at first [then] switch over to English with accent [and] JACK 2 [who] answered in English with British accent.

The intercepted radio chatter may have been related to joint British and EGAF flights over north-east Sinai.

END OF DAY 13

1545–1800	1	1305	Lahat	Dov Field Beer Sheba Dov Field
1612–1650	3	0409	Moller	Tel Nof Dov Field
1615–1645	1	0602	Solarsh	test
1623–1657	3	0108	Navot	training
1627–1735	106	RX-130	Lewis	test (two flights)
1650–1707	35	1101	Dougherty	test
1720–1725	101	2016/21	Goodlin	Tel Nof Hatzor delivery to Squadron 101
1750–2310	103	1403	Shatkai	Tel Nof Sodom Tel Nof Sodom Tel Nof
1755–1822	3	0405	Navot	training
1820–2145	1	1301	Solarsh	Dov Field Beer Sheba Dov Field
2010–2210	1	1305	Renov	Dov FieldBeer Sheba Dov Field

This is - reportedly - a photo taken during the Squadron 69 Rafah bombing mission on 4 January 1949; a total of about 24 bomb explosions can be counted in this image.

Slick Goodlin ferried Spitfire 2016 from Tel Nof to Hatzor, on delivery to Squadron 101, on 4 January 1949. Squadron 101 coded Spitfire 2016 as 21 and until the ceasefire the Spitfire - photographed flying over Hatzor - flew three missions, participated in two air combats and was credited with one kill.

2224–0007	106	RX-131	Keren attack Gaza with 24★A50+AI3 bombs
2225–0250	1	1301	Ospovat Dov Field Beer Sheba Dov Field
2310–0040	103	1401	Boshes Nathan Segal Kemp attack Faluja with 16★A100kg bombs

The ILDF advance in the direction of Rafah was slow; Egyptian defense was stiff. The ILAF launched two bombing sorties from sunset at 1653 until midnight. RX-131 was over Gaza from 2350 until 2352 and flew two runs, but did not observe strikes due to haziness; there was no AAA fire and Egyptian searchlights came on only after explosion of the first bombs. 1401 was over Faluja from 2350 until midnight, reported very good visibility over target and flew two runs at 4,000 feet; there was no AAA fire.

DAY 14
5 JANUARY 1949

Israel pressed ahead with its attack against Rafah; Egypt started to seek a ceasefire in order to stop Israel's momentum; Britain still meddled, as indicated in a meeting in Washington between the USA

Acting Secretary of State and the British Ambassador:

> The British Ambassador said that Mr Bevin, in view of the very great strategic interests of both USA and UK in the Near East and in light of necessity for an adequate defense in depth of Suez Canal, very much hoped that USA might find its way clear to exert pressure on Israel to withdraw to the lines in the Negev established by the Acting Mediator after the adoption by the Security Council of its resolution of 4 November 1948. I told the British Ambassador that for a variety of reasons I did not feel that we could accede to Mr Bevin's request. While, in an exceptional case such as that when the incursion by Israeli forces into Egypt threatened a much more grave conflict outside the boundaries of Palestine, we had been willing to make strong representations... Furthermore, we had found in practice that strong representations, to be effective, should be used sparingly; otherwise notes often were merely interesting documents for the archives but useful for no other purpose. [FRUS]

HARASS FALUJA

0133–0306	103	1405	Rosin Berliand Pozkanzner	
			attack Faluja with 16*A100+30*AI3 bombs	
			Greenberger Hollander Stern	
0136–0348	103	1403	Shatkai	Tel Nof Sodom Tel Nof
0511–0631	103	1405	Rosin Berliand Pozkanzner	
			attack Faluja with 16*A100+30*AI3 bombs	
			Greenberger Hollander Stern	

1405 was over Faluja from 0210 until 0220, reported good weather, good visibility, no AAA and bombed from 3,500 feet in three runs:

> Run 1 [heading] 120... 24 AI3s... two A100s; Run 2 eight A100s and six AI3s; Run 3 six A100s; all bombs seen to explode on approximately center of town where two [ILDF search]lights converged... Suggest one searchlight should sweep target while second remains stationary. Small arms fire directed against aircraft.

1405 was again over Faluja from 0540 to 0545, possibly later than the planned TOT – sunrise was at 0639 – reported good weather, good visibility, no AAA and bombed from 3,500 feet:

> One run made over target at heading of 150. Bombs released from racks in rapid succession and all incendiaries thrown... due to coming daylight... Bombs fell in western area of town; one incendiary started a fairly large fire and one appeared to be burning in a trench. Searchlights observed from very far out; kept on until aircraft reached target area; had to flash [aircraft] lights for them to be put on again.

RAID KHAN YUNES

0635–0704	35	1101	Dougherty	
			attack Khan Yunes with 8*50kg bombs	
0636–0730	35	1102	Soltau	ditto
0637–0731	35	1106	Gibson	ditto

A Squadron 101 clipped wing Spitfire undergoing maintenance, probably at Hatzor during the winter of 1948 to 1949. Squadron 101 seemingly had plenty of pilots and enough aircraft to mount much more than the average of some 10 sorties per day as actually flown during HOREV.

Squadron 69's lead ship - B-17 1601 - was adorned, post-war, with 33 mission markings on both the left and right sides of its nose section, though the arrangement of these markings varied from side to side. In any case the number of recorded missions that B-17 1601 flew during the Israeli War for Independence is 46, but was surely more than 50, as the July 1948 missions were not properly recorded.

0645–0822	101	2008/15	Augarten	escort Flight 35
0645–0822	101	2003/12	Peake	ditto

Gibson and Soltau were over Khan Yunes from 0710 until 0711:

> Visibility was good. Bombs were dropped on a vehicle concentration but no hits were seen. Bombs were also dropped across southern part of town. Explosions were seen about 30 seconds after leaving target...

Dougherty diverted to the alternative target of Faluja, was over the target from 0700 until 0701 and dropped all bombs in a single run:

> All bombs exploded and seemed to be direct hits on a 25-lb gun position.

The escorts reported excellent visibility as well as:

> Picked up AT-6s over field; only two bombed south-west of Khan Yunes in some orchards. From Khan Yunes near main road Rafah/ El Arish... Flew to Bir Masaid... small [air]field there; six [aircraft] dummies there; bombed them and on strafing run observed they were dummies. Flew to small field south of El Arish on deck; burnt out FIAT one kilometer north

of small field; two men hanging around FIAT. Then flew down along main road to Abu Ageila... concentration of 60-plus vehicles dispersed on both sides of road [from Abu Ageila to Auja]...; got heavy flak there. Then north...

RAID EL ARISH

Time	Sqn	A/C	Pilot	Route/Notes
0650–0935	1	1301	Renov	Dov Field Beer Sheba Dov Field
0732–	3	0407	Lee	Tel Nof Dov Field
0736–0758	3	0114	Biram	Tel Nof Dov Field
0843–0858	35	1101	Dougherty	test
0845–	3	0409	Hirsh	
0846–1040	69	1601	Raisin Goldstein Harris Cuburnek attack El Arish with 10★250kg bombs Aronson Goldstein Lichtman Duboff Meyerson Gershaw Gershenson	
0855–1200	1	1305	Kaplan	Dov Field Tel Nof Beer Sheba Dov Field
0902–0908	101	2012/16	Feldman	escort Squadron 69
0902–1044	101	2013/18	Schroeder	ditto
0917–1044	101	2002/11	Sinclair	ditto

1601 was over El Arish marshaling yards from 0947 until 0953, reported clear weather – 20 to 30 miles visibility over target – accurate AAA that caused a little hole in the tail and bombing from 14,500 feet, with bombs falling south-east of target. An Egyptian dummy air base was also reported:

An airfield, four fighter-type aircraft dispersed [but] no visible landing strip, believed to be at Bir Masaid.

The B-17 actually attacked unescorted, since Seymour Feldman aborted his escort, RTB and was replaced by Lee Sinclair:

Aircraft circled rendezvous for some time but did not connect with B-17s. Then proceeded direct to El Arish town via sea. Observed no signs of our bombing. Low-lying hazy smoke was seen over Gaza and thick white smoke up to 1,000 feet over Faluja...

EGYPT SEEKS CEASEFIRE

Time	Sqn	A/C	Pilot	Notes
1000–1129	35	Bet55 /0804	Dougherty	training
1030–1130	1	0412	Avira	training
1030–1340	1	1301	Steinman	Dov Field Beer Sheba Dov Field

USA Special Representative in Israel James McDonald reported from Tel Aviv, at 1100, a seemingly unbiased view of situation:

Thus, irrespective of what the precise intent was in instructing me to make those representations [of aforementioned USA-UK ultimatum], the deduction of Israel that, by forcing Israel abandon an obviously successful military action (which would have, in mind army and public here, neutralized a forward Egyptian base from which Egypt has during six months repeatedly launched destructive air and other attacks against Israel without occasioning any recorded direct complaint by US or UK), US is now directly involved in results of action it has taken. If Egyptian attacks should continue, or misunderstanding our action encourages Iraqi attack... US position will be compared here to Britain as power whose repeated maneuvers are having effect of letting Israel bleed to death by forcing her into position where she is neither free to end the war militarily nor obtain peace by negotiation...

The military facts... are that, owing [to] our representations, Israel forces have abruptly retreated from Egyptian territory, abandoning control roads. The tactics of ILDF apparently were to have raided El Arish and attack Rafah and neutralize them, then withdraw to open path for estimated 18,000 Egyptian troops to escape home to Egypt. Now situation very confused but it appears that the new position of Israeli forces has blocked escape route of Egyptians while leaving Rafah as yet untouched but completely cut off from northeast and southeast. This is what [USA] Mission [to Israel] meant when it ascribed "serious responsibility" arising out of US representations. [FRUS]

Unknown, yet, to Israel, Egypt – grasping the grave situation of the EGDF expeditionary force in the Gaza Strip and wishing to avoid a second Faluja Pocket – had already started to seek a ceasefire, as indicated in a message from the USA Acting Secretary of State that was wired to the USA Embassy in Cairo at about the same time:

Acting Palestine Mediator has informed us that his Representative in Cairo telephoned on 4 January [1949] that Egypt had confidentially notified him of its readiness to enter into talks with Israel on all outstanding questions under UN auspices provided Israel obeys... ceasefire order by 1400 GMT 5 January [1949].

Prior to HOREV, Flight 35 operated a handful of C-64s as a light transport element of the Tel Nof-based ILAF Air Transport Command (ATC). ILAF ATC then transformed into Squadron 106 and Flight 35 converted from C-64 to T-6 - even though small-scale operations of C-64 continued. The only C-64 to fly during HOREV was 0804, which Flight 35 still referred to in its pre-November 1948 ILAF identity as Bet55.

Squadron 101 P-51 2301/40 (right) and Spitfire 2003/12 (left) as photographed at Hatzor during the winter of 1948 to 1949. Boris Senior flew 2301 and Seymour Feldman flew 2003 during air combat on 5 January 1949.

The Egyptian-set timeframe was too short to be implemented but, not yet known to Israel, HOREV had finally forced Egypt to abandon its hardline policy and to agree to negotiation with Israel.

FIAT PRANG

1103–1243	101	2301/40	Senior	scramble
1103–1243	101	2003/12	Feldman	scramble

Reportedly, the EGAF no longer operated from air bases in Sinai, which were evacuated, and was granted British permission to refuel at RAF stations in the Suez Canal Zone. This probably complicated and disrupted EGAF operations, but the EGAF continued to attack the ILDF and occasionally the EGAF and ILAF engaged over the battlefield. Squadron 101 pilots Boris Senior and Seymour Feldman were scrambled to Rafah:

> Headed for Rafah over land. Patrolled Rafah/Auja road a few times; saw 40 vehicles heading to Rafah... encountering a lot of fire; a lot of Egyptian artillery firing on our vehicles. Then went to Abu Ageila and observed about 40 to 50 vehicles... scattered around road, well dispersed. Then along Abu Ageila road to El Arish and met a lot of flak, medium and heavy, fairly accurate, fairly intense at El Arish field. At El Arish field observed only one plane in a pen. Then headed towards Rafah inland from road and turned back to Rafah at Sheikh Noran. Came back at 7,500 feet and just off Rafah sighted three FIATs 500 to 1,000 feet below us. They were coming out of the sun preparatory to bombing dive. We came onto them out of the sun. Dogfight ensued. They jettisoned their bombs when they saw us. FIAT Number 1 headed right for home.
> Senior: made one pass at FIAT Number 3, he was turning. Made one pass and pulled out above and to his side. Then observed him diving down southwards pouring gray and black smoke. Then FIAT Number 2, in turning away from attack on Feldman, headed straight for me. I got three or four head-on bursts during ensuing dogfight but was not able to observe any strikes, but I am certain there were strikes. Observed him to roll and pour black smoke and a lot of glycol and dive down on his back. Followed him down and saw him prang... Believe other FIAT Number 3 did not return home.
> Feldman: Picked FIAT Number 2; jumped him. First shot full 90 degrees deflection; observed strikes on motor. Black smoke started to pour. He staged fighting. Followed him around in one complete loop and saw strikes in wing roots. Did two head-on attacks and observed strikes on engine again. Then Boris made four passes. Then followed him down firing steadily into him. Observed him prang with black and white smoke pouring out.

Both pilots thus saw the same, single enemy aircraft crashing in what seemed to be a shared kill. ILAFI Condensed Operational Summary Number 8 concluded:

> Two of our Spitfires engaged enemy FIAT fighter planes above Rafah. One Egyptian FIAT was definitely shot down while another was a probable.

The ILDF subsequently, on 9 January, confirmed the kill:

> On 5 January 1949 a FIAT was shot down by a Spitfire and a P-51 of ours. Negev Intelligence reports that it crashed 600 meters from our positions... within enemy defense lines.

The ILAF credited each pilot with a kill, thus a total claim of two.

PATROL

1110–1245	3	0108	Brown	Tel Nof Hatzor Tel Nof
1110–1405	1	0603	Avisar	Dov Field Beer Sheba Dov Field
1124–	3	0114	Biram	
12 17–1254	35	Bet55/0804	Soltau	Tel Nof Dov Field Tel Nof
1249–1447	3	0409	Hirsh	observation Faluja
1259–	3	0405	Navot	
1300–1428	101	2002/11	Wilson	patrol
1300–1428	101	2008/15	Goodlin	patrol

Wilson and Goodlin patrolled from Beer Sheba to Auja, Rafah and Faluja, did not observe any unusual activity and reported intense AAA fire over Rafah.

RAID RAFAH

1315–1400	1	1305	Solarsh	Dov Field Beer Sheba Dov Field
1400–1410	1	1301	Ospovat	test
1400–1420	1	1306	Kaplan	test
1410–1605	1	1302	Kaplan	Dov Field Ramat David DovField
1450–1735	1	1301	Ospovat	Dov Field Beer Sheba Dov Field
1500–1504	3	0114	Biram	test
1505–1655	69	1603	Noach Maseng Jacobs Michel Majzels attack Rafah with 10*A250 bombs Swiel Kahn Spicehandler Jacobson Hill Joffe	
1506–1654	69	1601	Raisin Ben Porat Harris Cuburnek attack Rafah with 10*A250+2*A100 bombs Lichtman Goldstein Aronson Duboff Meyerson Gershaw Gershenson	
1520–1643	35	1105	Black	test
1522–1630	101	2002/11	Dangott	escort Squadron 69
1522–1630	101	2008/15	Jacobs	ditto

DAY 14: 5 JANUARY 1949

Squadron 69 B-17 1603 - still painted as 693 for the third B-17 of Squadron 69 - as photographed right through the 0.5-inch Browning sight of a fellow Hammer; 1603 bombed Rafah during the HOREV Day 14 afternoon mission.

Squadron 1 flew two Bonanzas - 0602 and 0603 - for liaison between ILAF bases. Though equipped with bomb racks, and formerly used as bombers, the Squadron 1 Bonanza did not fly offensive missions during HOREV.

Squadron 69 returned to Rafah target 2 and target 3, which the B-17s had missed the previous day. Fair to good weather welcomed the bombers over Rafah from 1555 until 1559 (1601) and from 1557 to 1557 (1603) at 15,500 feet (both). Crews reported AAA as less than expected and not up to Rafah standard. Lead bombardier Jules Cuburnek reported:

> Buildings hit to the right side of target 2... three distinct columns of smoke were seen spreading; these columns could be seen from over Tel Aviv.

ISRAEL AGREES TO CEASEFIRE

1547–	3	0106	Biram	
1556 –1702	3	0110	Ruff	Tel Nof Haifa
1602–	3	0407		
1621–1715	106	RX-130	Christiernsson	training
1635–1705	1	0603	Avisar Kaplan	training

USA Special Representative in Israel James McDonald's message prompted a softer-tone reply from the USA Secretary of State:

> Please... express USA gratification on learning... that no Israeli troops now remain on Egyptian territory. Please add that USA is relieved that danger of much more serious conflict in Middle East has been averted. ILFM must realize representations [of US-UK ultimatum] were motivated by sincere friendship of USA for Israel... [USA] has been informed... that Egypt had confidentially notified UN... it was willing to enter into talks with Israel under UN auspices on all outstanding questions, provided Israel will obey... ceasefire... by 1400 GMT 5 January [1949]. Although this info reached USA after this deadline had expired, USA in friendly spirit desires to acquaint Israel of foregoing info with trust that it may still be possible for Israel and Egypt to enter into negotiations following a prompt and effective ceasefire. [FRUS]

Israel decided, during the afternoon, to agree to a ceasefire.

HARASS FALUJA/GAZA

| 1750–1920 | 103 | 1405 | Agmon Keidar Laron Manor |
| | | | attack Faluja with 16*A100+25*AI3 bombs |

An ILAF C-46 in flight over Tel Aviv later in 1949. During HOREV, Squadron 106 mostly bombed Gaza but also flew VELVETTA 2 missions to Yugoslavia.

			Berger Pinto Greenberger
1805–	3	0405	Machnes
1925–2020	106	RX-131	Foster
			attack Gaza with 24*A50+AI3 bombs
1930–2055	103	1401	Boshes Nathan Segal Kemp
			attack Faluja with 16*A100 bombs
2045–2135	106	RX-137	Christiernsson
			attack Gaza with 24*A50+AI3 bombs
2150–2330	103	1405	Katz Laron Manor
			attack Faluja with 16*A100+25*AI3 bombs
			Hollander Berger Pinto
2215–2315	106	RX-131	Foster
			attack Gaza with 24*A50+AI3 bombs
2215–0115	1	1301	Lahat Dov Field Beer Sheba Dov Field

1405 was over Faluja from 1830 until 1841, reported good weather, very good visibility, no AAA and two bombing runs – headings 130 and 120 – at 4,000 feet.

An unidentified enemy aircraft, possibly an EGAF Stirling, bombed Lod Airport at 1915; the ILDF reported that four bombs were dropped and that three people were injured, while the ILPM wrote in his diary:

> I was informed that Lod Airport was bombed and that Battalion 82 mess was hit; one soldier was killed and two were injured.

RX-131 was over Gaza from 1950 until 1955, reported fair visibility and flew two bombing runs:

> On first, dropped five bombs which fell around center of town. On second, 18 bombs and five boxes of AI3s were dropped which fell on south-west edge of target. One bomb was not dropped. No fires were observed after bomb drop. Light, inaccurate AAA was encountered and four searchlights, radar-controlled; these lights are on north-west side of target.

1401 was over Faluja from 2009 until 2013, reported very good weather, very good visibility and bombed in two runs – headings 120 and 130 – from 3,000 feet.

RX-137 was over Gaza from 2115 until 2125, reported very good visibility and flew two bombing runs:

> On the first, 13 bombs were dropped and fell along the road running from center of town towards coast; one large and two small fires were observed burning to west and in center of town. On second run, 11 bombs and five boxes of AI3s were dropped; they fell on north-east side of target; one large and one small fire were observed on north-east side of target. Accurate searchlights were observed on north-east corner of target. Medium, inaccurate AAA fire was encountered.

1405 was again over Faluja from 2230 until 2241, reported good weather, very good visibility and flew two bombing runs – both headings 110 – at 4,000 feet.

RX-131 returned to Gaza from 2237 until 2245, reported good visibility and flew two bombing runs:

> On the first, eight bombs were dropped and were seen falling on south/south-east corner of town; 16 bombs and five boxes of AI3s were dropped on second, all were observed exploding. Seven searchlights were observed on south-east side of target. No fires were observed. Light and inaccurate 40mm AAA fire was encountered.

DAY 15
6 JANUARY 1949

Egypt and Israel agreed to a ceasefire: Egypt, because it was losing the battle; Israel, in spite of HOREV, because of failure to accomplish its objective to defeat EGDF in Israel. The ILPM wrote in his diary:

> This arrangement [ceasefire] will result in EGDF remaining in Gaza [Strip] and Faluja Pocket will not be eliminated but nevertheless this is a huge accomplishment: an important step along path to peace and strengthening of Israel's position. If we will reach an agreement with Egypt then it will be easier to reach agreement with Jordan and the others [Arab nations]...

HARASS FALUJA

0145–0330   103   1405   Katz Laron Manor
                         attack Faluja with
16*A100+25*AI3   bombs
                         Hollander Pinto

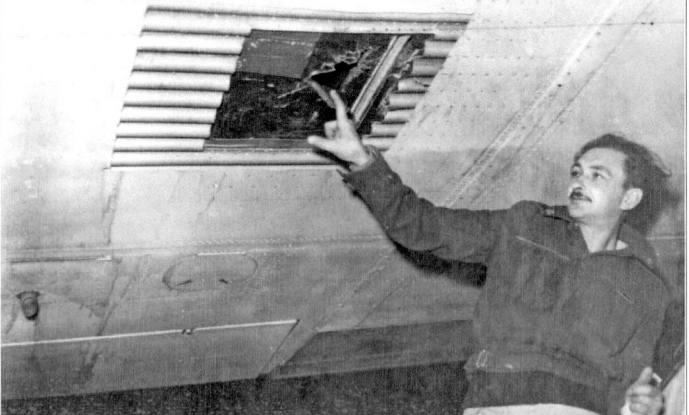

A Squadron 69 serviceman points at AAA damage to a B-17; EGDF AAA was very active throughout HOREV, but did not down ILAF aircraft.

0310–0440   103   1401   Boshes Nathan Segal Kemp
                         attack Faluja with 16*A100 bombs

Meanwhile, hostilities continued. Front D's plan for the night of 5 to 6 January called for Brigade 10 to attack and occupy fortifications around the crossroads south-east of Rafah so that Brigade 8 would pass through and attack Rafah camp and town during 6 January.

1405 was over Faluja from 0228 until 0241, reported good weather, good visibility, no AAA and bombed from 4,000 feet in two runs; the first, heading 120; the second, heading 130. 1401 was over Faluja from 0348 until 0352, reported good weather, excellent visibility, no AAA fire and bombed from 3,000 feet in two runs; both headings 120.

PATROL SOUTH

0645–0810   101   2018/15   Cohen   patrol
0645–0810   101   2013/18   Ruch   patrol

Brigade 10's night-time attack failed, so Front D ordered Brigade 8 to attack the crossroads during daylight, but ILDF and ILAF operations started to slow down due to deteriorating weather:

> Visibility was poor. Aircraft patrolled Rafah, Gaza and El Arish area; no vehicular movement was observed. On El Arish/Abu Ageila road, a petrol bowser was seen turning off El Arish road into Auja road. Aircraft made several strafing passes at bowser, which was finally set on fire. Heavy and fairly accurate flak was encountered from El Arish; slight and medium flak from Gaza.

RAID RAFAH

0714–1405   3   0108   Giladi   Tel Nof Dov Field
                                          Tel Nof
0755–0914   101   2008/15   Dangott   escort Squadron 69
0755–0914   101   2002/11   Schroeder   ditto
0755–0930   69   1601   Raisin Ben Porat Harris Cuburnek
                             attack Rafah with 16*A100 bombs
                             Lichtman Goldstein Aronson Duboff
                             Meyerson Gershaw Gershenson

1601 was over Rafah from 0833 until 0836; the crew reported good weather and good visibility but sand haze over the target, and flew a single bombing run, heading 315, at 16,000 feet in face of heavy and medium but inaccurate AAA fire. Al Raisin commented:

> Cannot communicate with fighters, ships or base; can something be done about contact? It is suggested that target

DAY 15: 6 JANUARY 1949

Squadron 69 bombardier Jules Cuburnek suggested - in the wake of the 6 January 1949 morning raid - that ILAFHQ should use Yarden Hotel (one of two hotels in Tel Aviv confiscated for ILAFHQ, the other being the Yarkon Hotel) as reference for an optimal bombing target.

Squadron 101 pilots Lee Sinclair (left) and Aaron Finkel (right) in front of S199 1906 at Hatzor. Both missed the start of HOREV due to participation in VELVETTA 2, so Sinclair flew only six missions during HOREV and Finkel four missions.

> to be attacked be chosen well in advance of proposed take-off time and not in the last moment [with] insufficient information as to target; briefing folder says area contains well but nothing else is mentioned.

Meanwhile, bombardier Jules Cuburnek pointed his sights at ILAF HQ which, at the time, was based at Yarden Hotel in Tel Aviv:

> Had no target photo; almost impossible to identify aiming point. However, with excellent cooperation from navigator [John Harris], identified it. The target covered too big an area. Next time give us a smaller area about the size of... Yarden Hotel.

The escorts reported:

> Visibility was very good. Bombers were escorted to Rafah and bombs were observed to fall in built-up area, north of Rafah station. Then aircraft escorted B-17s back to meeting point and returned to patrol Gaza area. Heavy, inaccurate flak was encountered from Rafah.

ROCKETRY TRAIN

0844–1721	35	Bet55 /0804	Gibson	Tel Nof Dov Field Tel Nof
0930–1015	1	1306	Steinman	Dov Field Beer Sheba
1000–1100	2	0401		photo Gaza Strip
1030–1146	3	0407	Hirsh	observation
1050–1240	3	0405	(BarAv)	training
1115–1320	1	1302	Renov	Dov Field Ramat David Dov Field
1137–1250	101	2008/15	Wilson	attack train
1137–1250	101	2302/41	Goodlin	ditto

0401 and 0407 reported good and very good visibility, but the weather was indeed getting worse, to the point that Squadron 101 pilots could not attack a train:

> The [P-51] load consisted of six rockets. Visibility was very poor. Aircraft was to have attacked a reported train between Rafah and El Arish... This could not be carried out owing to dust covering area. On El Arish/AbuAgeila road, a truck, five kilometers out of Abu Ageila, was observed heading to El Arish; five rockets were fired at the truck with no apparent result. Each aircraft strafed truck and strikes were observed during both attacks... A convoy was observed... heading to El Arish; the trucks at the end [of convoy] were strafed and were observed to blow up, believed to have carried ammunition; the vehicles of the convoy... were spread 200 feet apart. Observed large number of [ILDF] vehicles moving from Auja to Rafah.

VERY POOR VISIBILITY

1317–1507	3	0407	Hirsh	observation Judea
1335–1451	101	2002/11	Augarten	patrol
1335–1451	101	2013/18	Feldman	patrol

Augarten and Feldman reported very poor visibility during the patrol from El Arish to Abu Ageila and Bir Hama:

> At... a half-track was seen carrying troops and at... a... vehicle was seen carrying troops. Both... were proceeding to Abu Ageila. Both... were strafed and damaged but did not burn.

ALASKAN C-46 OVER NEGEV

1427–1607	3	0405	Rosen	Tel Nof Dov Field Tel Nof
1456–1557	101	2003/12	Senior	patrol
1456–1557	101	2012/16	Sinclair	patrol

Senior and Sinclair reported poor visibility south of Beer Sheba:

> ...between Beer Sheba and Nevatim... an Alaskan Airways C-46 was seen heading north at a height of 6,000 feet...

HARASS GAZA

1515–1552	35	1105	Flint	test
1620–1740	1	0603	Renov	Dov Field Tel Nof Beer Sheba Dov Field

The ILAF suspended Flying School courses in preparation for HOREV. Advance training air cadets were assigned to liaison squadrons as pilots, while primary training air cadets were assigned to transport squadrons as bomb chuckers. A C-46 crew of a HOREV Day 15 bombing mission number 11 to 12; air cadet Benjamin Peled - ILAF Commander 1973 to 1977 - was assigned to Squadron 106 as C-46 bomb chucker.

1705–1805	106	1701	Lewis	training
1747–1915	106	1704	Ford Henenson	
			attack Gaza with 24*50kg+10*41lb+ AI3 bombs	
1902–2040	106	1707	Keren	ditto
2135–2240	106	1704	Ford/Henenson	
			attack Gaza with 24*A50+AI3 bombs	
2228–2320	106	1707	Keren	ditto

Brigade 8's daylight attack also failed to occupy the Rafah crossroads so Front D launched yet another night-time effort to cut the road from the Sinai Peninsula to Gaza Strip, with ILAF support limited to harassment of Gaza. 1704 was over Gaza from 1818 until 1835, reported very good visibility and flew two bombing runs:

> On the first, 10 bombs were dropped along road to center of town. On the second, 13 50-kilogram bombs, 15 AI3s and 10 41-lb bombs were dropped, falling across center of town. Fire and three large explosions, bright yellow in color, were seen. Observed three to four searchlights north of town; they were accurate. Encountered seven bursts of AAA fire, fairly accurate.

1707 was over Gaza from 2000 until 2010, reported good visibility and flew two runs:

> On the first [run], 14 A50 and all incendiary bombs were dropped across town. On the second [run], remaining 10 A50s were dropped across town. Fires were then observed from first run. Explosions were heard but were not observed. Encountered five bursts from AAA, apparently not less than 75mm caliber; the bursts were rapid and accurate.

1704 was again over Gaza from 2230 until 2245, reported good visibility and flew two bombing runs.

1707 returned to Gaza from 2255 to 2305, reported good visibility and flew two bombing runs.

END OF DAY 15

A sandstorm slowed down ILDF and ILAF operations during Day 15; from sunrise at 0639 until sunset at 1655, the ILAF launched only one bombing sortie plus two escort sorties and eight patrol sorties.

The UN-mediated ceasefire was set for 1200 GMT, 1400 local time, on 7 January 1949, but the UK still meddled, as the UK Embassy in Washington reported to the USA State Department:

> The British Embassy... also stated that a RAF reconnaissance on 4 January [1949] showed a party of 30 Israeli troops still occupying a strongpoint within Egyptian territory six miles west of Auja. Photographs taken on this reconnaissance revealed that an anti-tank ditch had been bulldozed across the road one mile west of the strongpoint and five miles inside Egypt. Three anti-tank guns were observed in position at the strongpoint.

DAY 16
7 JANUARY 1949

The weather improved and both sides intensified operations in order to improve their positions by the ceasefire at 1400. Front D's night-time attack succeeded in cutting the main road from Sinai to Gaza at a point west of the Rafah crossroads.

RAID RAFAH

0705–0850	69	1603	McConville Ratushniak Seftel	
			attack Rafah with 16*A100 bombs	
			Weinstein Kahn Schwartzbach	
			Wadman	
			Kaplan Robinson Liponetzky Cohen	
0707–0845	69	1601	Feldman Ben Porat	
			Bresslof Weissbrod	
			Fink Dinkin Soltan Lazarus Nash	
			Jackson	
0730–0844	101	2008/15	McElroy	escort Squadron 69
0730–0844	101	2013/18	Sinclair	ditto

Squadron 69 crews reported good weather and heavy, accurate AAA fire; 1601 was over the target from 0755 to 0756 and 1603 followed from 0804 until 0805. Both flew a single run – 1601 heading 330 and 1603 heading 320 – and bombed from 15,000 feet. The designated target was missed but the raid was rated successful:

> As area is full of troops and tents, some damage must have been caused, although original target is left undamaged.

Rafah was the target that B-17 1603 bombed on its first and last Israeli War for Independence missions on 15 July 1948 and 7 January 1949.

Squadron 101 pilot Jack Doyle escorted Flight 35 to bomb Faluja on 7 January 1949 in Spitfire 2003, which Squadron 101 coded 12; the Squadron 101 code was painted over the ILAF number.

Squadron 101 pilot Boris Senior and P-51 TINK - 2301 - at Hatzor during the winter of 1948 to 1949.

Egyptian AAA fire damaged both bombers; 1601 was hit in the left wing, 1603 in the tail. The escorts concluded:

> Met two Forts at 10,000 feet right on time... out to sea... inland past Gaza and came in on target... made one run, proceeded out to sea... went home parallel with coast; left them off Gaza. In bombing, Forts overshot dumps due west of marshaling yards and set what appeared to be... buildings on fire. Then returned to Rafah/Auja main road... saw 100 vehicles well dispersed on and on both sides of road...

RAID KHAN YUNES

0729–0827	35	1106	Gibson	attack Khan Yunes with 8*50kg bombs
0729–0827	35	1101	Baker	ditto
0729–0827	35	1102	Soltau	ditto
0729–0827	35	1105	Flint	ditto
0729–0827	35	1107	Black	ditto
0735–0825	101	2003/12	Doyle	escort Flight 35
0735–0825	101	2012/16	Peake	ditto

Flight 35 was over Khan Yunes from 0749 until 0750 and reported good visibility. ILAFI reported:

> Each aircraft made one run over target and 32 bombs were dropped, in each case in two sets of four. The eight bombs in one of the aircraft hang up and this aircraft landed bombed-up. All bombs fell north-west across target area. Strafing was also carried out in general area of police station. All bombs dropped exploded. No AAA fire was reported.

The escorts possibly confused the target, as ILAFI reported:

> Picked up five AT-6s over home base; had been sitting in cockpit for one hour and 20 minutes. Escorted them to target Rafah. As Harvards started bombing, Spit Number 2 reported bogies. Climbed to intercept; they were our two Spits escorting B-17s. Harvards bombed north part of Rafah town; observed bombs to fall in area of town... Spit Number 2 had rough engine so we turned home...

TRAIN STILL ACTIVE

0828–	3	0405	Giladi	Tel Nof Dov Field
0845–1135	1	1302	Efrat	Dov Field Ramat David Tel Nof Dov Field Ramat David Dov Field
0910–1045	1	0412	Ospovat	training
0915–1020	1	0701	Lavi	training
0940–1000	1	1307	Kaplan	test
0950–1130	101	2012/16	Augarten	patrol
0950–1130	101	2003/12	Feldman	patrol
0951–1111	3	0114	Ruff	observation Faluja

After all the ILAF efforts to cut the railroad and stop train movements, the Egyptian railway was still active, even during daylight, as Squadron 101 pilots reported:

> Told... to investigate bogies at Rafah... Then over to Abu Ageila/El Arish road and observed train moving to El Arish approximately two to three miles east of El Arish, about 10 cars. Then down to Abu Ageila along main road from El Arish.

Augarten and Feldman strafed two trucks along the Abu Ageila/El Arish road. The first truck burst into flames and the second blew-up.

RAID DIR BALAH

1050–1300	3	0405		leaflets photo (Lebanon)
1050–1125	35	1106	Gibson	attack DirBalah with 8*50kg bombs
1050–1125	35	1101	Baker	ditto

1050–1125	35	1102	Soltau	ditto	
1050–1125	35	1105	Dougherty	ditto	
1050–1125	35	1107	Black	ditto	
1050–1225	101	2301/40	Senior	escort Flight 35	
1050–1225	101	2302/41	Doyle	ditto	

Flight 35 was over Dir Balah from 1110 until 1111. The Squadron 101 debrief from 1245 stated:

> Escorted five Harvards to Dir Balah, observed their bombs hit in north-east and north-west sectors of town. Escorted them back to near our field. Then headed towards Rafah. From Rafah, along main road, to Auja. Observed scattered transport. Then back to Rafah. Headed southward and observed two fighters... Turned around to get on their tails and lost them due to poor visibility. Spent another 10 minutes looking for them. Next saw six fighters on deck, heading towards Rafah, about 18 miles from Rafah on Rafah/Auja road.
> Boris [Senior]: Throttle back and went down in steep spiral getting onto their tails. Came out above and behind them. Fired four bursts and pulled up to side and saw another aircraft circling towards me to north. Full throttle and climbed up. Turned to right and lost all in haze. Lost contact with my Number 2 from the time we entered the fight. Met Doyle again north of Rafah, near Dir Balah. Closing speed too fast to determine whether I got strikes or not.
> Doyle: Dive down... made one pass, fired at one aircraft... ended in middle of their formation. Pulled up to starboard. Made second pass at another aircraft and pulled out again to starboard and observed aircraft strafing road. After... first pass, saw two aircraft pulling into Boris. Went down on aircraft strafing road. Started firing from 700 yards; strikes in wing, wing cowling came off, strikes on engine and fuselage. Aircraft went away pouring brown and black smoke. Broke off and climbed up. Met Boris north of Rafah and came home.

Additionally, at 1930, Squadron 101 pilot Jack Doyle was debriefed again:

> Went out with Boris Senior, picked up T-6s over base, went on to target Dir Balah. Bombs burst on side of target, went back to Hatzor with T-6s and then went down to Auja; flew around looking at roads; scattered transport on roads. Boris sights aircraft, informs me on radio. Were at about 5,000 feet; climbed into sun and attacked aircraft. Could not identify aircraft, neither nationality nor mark; aircraft were strafing roads when I saw them first. Aircraft were seven in number that Number 1 [Senior] saw going in one direction; I saw four to five aircraft in another direction. Dive down following Number 1, seemed to have passed Number 1 as he was circling. Made one pass at outside aircraft of formation. Speed of dive carried me into middle of formation; no strikes observed on first pass. Pulled starboard, chopped throttle, starting another pass. Made pass observing Number 1 being attacked by two aircraft; informed Number 1 on radio of two approaching aircraft on to him from starboard. Followed my second attack; fired and saw strikes from engine fuselage. Pulled up again and observed aircraft strafing road down at that point, dive down to him as I struck him. Observed piece of wing peel off, continued striking and then heard Number 1 on radio. By that time, aircraft smoking and going down. Engagement was in sandstorm. Had by that time only one gun firing. Number 1 arrived, this was north of Rafah, and from then turned on to base. Flak at Rafah still quite good.

The ILAF credited Senior with an EGAF Spitfire kill and Doyle with an EGAF FIAT kill, even though the pilots did not identify the type and nationality of aircraft and even though no enemy aircraft were seen to crash.

FOUR BRITISH SPITFIRES DOWN

1115–1205	1	0412	Kraft	training	
1136–1227	101	2008/15	McElroy	patrol	
1136–1227	101	2013/18	Goodlin	patrol	

British meddling continued, even though Israel posed no danger to the Suez Canal Zone and Egypt had already indicated that it had no intentions to invoke the 1936 Anglo-Egyptian Treaty. RAF Squadron 208 dispatched, at 1115, four Spitfires from Fayid to patrol over the road from Auja to Rafah; the road from Auja to Rafah was indeed, partially, west of the border, but Auja and Rafah were both east of the border, while the border was unmarked. The British briefing ordered the lead pair, Cooper and Close, to fly at 500 feet and the trailing pair, McElhaw and Sayers, to fly at 1,500 feet.

The Auja to Rafah road had just been the scene of an EGAF air raid and an air combat when the four British Spitfires appeared at low altitude, flying with external fuel tanks, over ILDF troops whom had just been attacked by enemy aircraft. The ILDF troops saw aircraft that were definitely not Israeli, mistook external fuel tanks for bombs, opened fire and hit the two lead, lower Spitfires. Close bailed out; Cooper climbed. It was probably at this point that McElroy and Goodlin arrived. Though subsequent reports vary, the debrief, at 1300, indicated:

> Heard British voices on radio and headed for our concentration on Auja/Rafah road. Observed smoke on ground from our burning transport... Saw Spit 16s hacking. Dived on them.
> McElroy: One Spit pulling up, climbing to port, second Spit just pulling up from deck. Formatted on them 25 to 30 feet to starboard. Observed it was enemy Spit; pointed wings, round fin and rudder. Closed my throttle, line up behind him; fired four seconds burst. Aircraft blew up and flew through debris, damaging my own kite. Turned back to find other enemy aircraft. Saw parachuting pilot hit ground, doff chute and run like hell heading west. Looked back to see my kite hit the deck one mile west of our transport. Headed home as my aircraft damaged.
> Goodlin: Upon seeing McElroy waggle his wings and dive, my radio unserviceable, and pulled off after him and only then saw two Spit 16s pulling up from strafing run. McElroy attacked second Spit and opened throttle to chase [other Spit] who climbed into sun. After reaching 7,000 feet, on his tail, he dived into me and commenced dicing. At this time he was close enough for me to see his markings; RAF roundels and tail stripes. We diced for five to seven minutes before I managed to get on his tail, during which time he fired a few wild bursts at me. On getting into firing position, I gave him a short burst... and observed immediate strikes on nose section and his propeller disintegrated. One more short burst and pieces flew off, followed by

CEASEFIRE

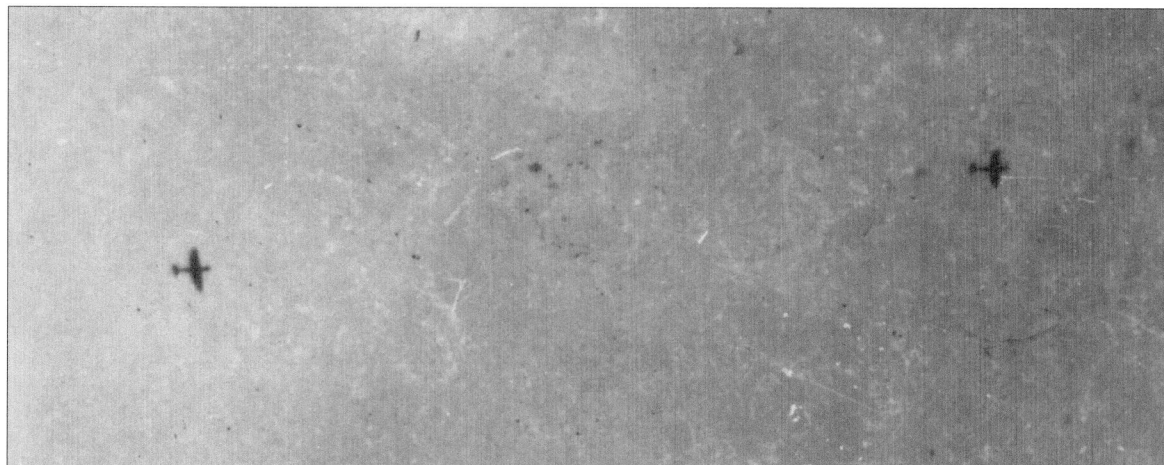

Reportedly taken during the 7 January 1949 morning engagement between British and Israeli fighters, this photo may have been taken prior to combat as it seems to capture the two round wingtipped Spitfires of the RAF Squadron 208's lower altitude section.

Squadron 101 pilot John McElroy standing beside the damaged tail section of Spitfire 2008 after combat on 7 January 1949.

RAF Squadron 208 pilot Timothy John McElhaw.

canopy, after which pilot bailed. Circled, looking for McElroy; then headed home. An initial ILDF statement was released on 8 January:

Israeli ground forces were strafed by enemy fighters in the morning. Israeli aircraft intercepted and in the ensuing battle one Egyptian FIAT was shot down. At the same time a number of Spitfire aircraft appeared over the battle area, flying low over Israeli troops who attacked them with anti-aircraft fire. One was shot down. Israeli fighter cover engaged a second Spitfire which was weaving low over Israeli forward positions and shot it down.

The pilot of the second aircraft bailed out and was captured by Israeli troops. He proved to be... Timothy John McElhaw... From documents in this pilot's possession and from interrogation, it transpires that on the morning of 7 January [1949] four pilots... were briefed for a mission... They were informed that a battle was in progress along the Egyptian Israeli frontier... and that very little was known by British HQ about the whereabouts of these troops and about the developments of the battle. The purpose of this sortie was an armed reconnaissance to photograph the battle area and the position of opposing troops and to bring back as much information as possible on the situation. The leading aircraft... was to photograph the Auja Rafah area. The guns in all aircraft were loaded... McElhaw states that they weaved low over the battle zone in accordance with normal tactical reconnaissance unit tactics. He saw one RAF aircraft hit by anti-aircraft fire and subsequently saw it crash. He was engaged shortly afterwards and shot down.

Actually, both Close and McElhaw bailed out over ILDF troops and were taken prisoners. Cooper ended up walking in the desert before meeting Egyptians, who transported him on a camel to El Arish, from where he was evacuated to Ismailia on a hospital train. Sayers was killed. The ILAF credited McElroy with one kill and Goodlin with one kill, while ILDF troops shot down the other two Spitfires.

SPOTTED EIGHT FIATS

1205–1217	103	1403	Wygle	test Tel Nof Tel Nof
1320–1408	101	2012/16	Wilson	patrol
1320–1408	101	2003/11	Ruch	patrol
1325–1430	1	0412	Hofshi Abarbanell	training
1333–1421	101	2016/21	Dangott	test

Intensified air activity over north-east Sinai continued as Wilson and Ruch patrolled over Rafah and El Arish:

Turned south to Abu Ageila, radio [message] from base informed us aircraft in area. Spotted eight FIATs... at 8,000 feet; we were at 8,500 feet... Passed them, they were heading east, we were heading west. Broke down onto tail end section, they were flying in sections of four. Three or four FIATS jettisoned their bombs into the sands. Fought with them. Wilson observed strikes on FIAT's starboard wing; fire out all his ammo. On way home observed three or four bombs straddling Rafah/Auja road... but could not find any aircraft.

Dangott reported unlimited visibility, as well as:

Was making local test hop over field and routed by radio [message] south to join Wilson and Ruch near El Arish. Orbited El Arish, Rafah and Gaza but made no contact with our aircraft or enemy aircraft.

CEASEFIRE

1400–1450	1	0701	Solarsh Lavi	training
1400–1605	3	0405		leaflets photo (Lebanon)
1411–1447	3	0407	Navot	training
1411–1503	101	2301/40	Augarten	patrol
1411–1503	101	2302/41	Peake	patrol

Fire should have ceased abruptly at 1400 but, as often happened in the Middle East, it took some time to fully implement the ceasefire. Augarten and Peake patrolled over Egyptian territory past the ceasefire, reporting good visibility and no activity:

> Headed right down for Rafah. Saw our concentration [of troops] on Rafah/Auja road. Straight down to Bir Hama, nothing there. Then on to Bir Masaid, dummy aircraft still there. Then flew over El Arish field, nothing there.

Nevertheless, the bulk of the fighting indeed ended at 1400 and ILDF Deputy Chief of Staff Yigael Yadin attended a press conference to sum up HOREV:

> ILAF had been extremely active and high tribute was paid by Yadin to their vital contribution. Apart from aircraft destroyed on ground by Israeli bombers, Israeli fighters had shot down some 12 Egyptian planes, two of them that very morning and one probable. No Israeli aircraft had been lost.

Yadin's statement was not accurate; one of the inaccuracies was reference to all aircraft engaged that morning as Egyptian; some were British and more British aircraft were already in the air, heading to north-east Sinai.

ONE BRITISH TEMPEST DOWN

1445–1640	1	1302	Efrat	Dov Field Ramat David Dov Field
1524–1612	1	0412	Porat	training
1530–1630	101	2016/21	Weizman	patrol
1530–1630	101	2003/12	Jacobs	patrol
1530–1630	101	2012/16	Dangott	patrol
1530–1630	101	2013/18	Schroeder	patrol

The disappearance of four Spitfires prompted a British search, with four Squadron 208 Spitfires flying at low level, seven Squadron 213 Tempests as medium cover at 6,000 feet and eight Squadron 213 Tempests at 10,000 feet as top cover. The British Spitfires and Tempests departed Fayid and Deversoir at around 1530.

At 1550 the Squadron 101 Spitfires arrived over Rafah, flying at 8,000 feet, and saw eight aircraft, type identified as Spitfire 16, flying at 6,000 feet. There were no other Israeli fighters in the air at the time, so the spotted aircraft were certainly not Israeli. The only thus far unearthed debrief from this flight is Dangott's but it was written in barely readable handwriting and deciphered as follows:

> ...unidentified aircraft over Israel territory... turned into them and they all turned into me. Identified aircraft as Spits, definitely RAF markings... engaged in dogfight with... Spit which started at 6,000 feet, spiral down to the deck right over Rafah station.

An ILDF soldier examines the wreckage of the British Tempest that Squadron 101 shot down on 7 January 1949.

An ILDF soldier points at the RAF roundel of the shot-down Tempest.

> I was on his tail, firing at him approximately... seconds in a turn to get any... on his plane for effective... We climbed up 2,000 feet, he pecked off turning south. Passed him, till I returned he was definitely... away. Dropped him, then turned starboard and saw another Spit about 2,000 feet turning into me. Turned into him and quickly... in... on his tail and opened up. Observed strikes on first and second aircraft.
> As soon as disengaged first aircraft, saw burning aircraft on deck. Second aircraft turned to west on deck and pulled up. Started climbing up again, at about 3,000 feet observed another below me. Turned into him. He did a complete spiral on deck and went down south. I get one gun only shooting at him. Climbed back to 4,000 feet... called leader, got no reply. Went near burning aircraft, could not identify and then went home.

A subsequent, 9 January 1949, ILAFI report integrated previous debriefs into a condensed summary:

> Visibility was fair. Flying west of Rafah at 8,000 feet, seven to eight unidentified aircraft were observed over Israel Territory. They were in battle formation, abreast, about 150 yards apart. The aircraft were observed to have RAF markings; they were silvery painted and had elliptical wings and at least one of the aircraft had a bomb on each wing. A dogfight ensued. The bombs were jettisoned. One explosion from a bomb was seen. Strikes were observed on at least three of the aircraft. One other aircraft was seen to go into a spin from which it did not

DAY	Faluja	Gaza	Khan Yunes	Rafah	El Arish	Dir Balah	Manshiya	other targets
		1★Piper(27)	1★C-47(1,600)					Auja 1★Beauf(180) and 4★T-6(1,600)
5 (27)		3★C-47(3,927)					6★T-6(2,400)	
6 (28)		4★B-17(7,350)					5★T-6(2,000)	
		2★C-47(3,200)						
		23★T-6(9,200)						
7 (29)		2★C-47(3,200)		3★B-17(5,100)	3★B-17(4,045)			
		13★T-6(5,200)						
8 (30)		3★C-47(4,330)						
		4★T-6(1,452)						
9 (31)	3★B-17(5,600)	3★C-46(3,825)				1★C-46(1,275)		Bir Hama 3★Spit(273)
		7★C-47(7,625)						
10 (1)	2★C-47(3,150)	2★C-46(2,550)						support ILNF 1★B-17(1,600)
		2★Spit(280)						
11 (2)	5★C-47(8,075)	3★C-46(3,825)	4★T-6(1,450)		6★B-17(9,600)			Bir Burg 2★Spit (280)
					2★Spit(280)			
12 (3)	4★C-47(6,655)	2★C-46(2,550)	6★T-6(2,400)	4★B-17(6,400)	2★Spit(280)	3★T-6(1,200)		
13 (4)	1★C-47(1,690)	2★B-17(3,600)	4★Spit(1,080)	2★B-17(3,950)				
	1★T-6(475)	1★C-46(1,275)		3★T-6(1,200)				
14 (5)	6★C-47(9,930)	3★C-46(3,825)		2★B-17(5,200)	1★B-17(2,500)			
15 (6)	2★C-47(3,275)	4★C-46(5,100)		1★B-17(1,600)	2★Spit(280)			
16 (7)			5★T-6(2,000)	2★B-17(3,200)		5★T-6(2,000)		
TOTAL	96 (89,704kg)	28 (36,570kg)	28 (14,239kg)	27 (41,726kg)	24 (29,012kg)	12 (5,564kg)	12 (4,544kg)	16 (4,645kg)

Absolute numbers were impressive, but the daily average was a mere 14 strike sorties and only 13,294 kilograms of bombs. The ILAF did not attack in preparation for ILDF attacks and did not fly close air support, while an analysis of ILAF bombings on Faluja concluded that damage was minor. It is highly unlikely that the EGAF evacuation of bases in north-east Sinai was a result of ILAF raids; it is more probable that the EGAF retreated from north-east Sinai for fear of ILDF occupation.

ILAF fighter operations were viewed as successful. Front D Commander Yigal Alon reported to the ILPM on 17 January 1949:

Our fighter operations were very efficient and almost only them hit our forces, three times!

Squadron 101 launched 160 sorties, mostly escorts and patrols, and during 10 missions enemy aircraft were engaged. The ILAF credited Squadron 101 pilots with 14 'kills' – seven Egyptian FIATs, three Egyptian Spitfires, one Egyptian Macchi, two British Spitfires and one British Tempest – but of these, only six were actually seen to crash, so the balance should be treated as probable kills until the emergence of materials which may approve or negate the 'kill' claims.

UN observers examining the wreckage of the British Tempest which Israel shot down on 7 January 1949.

recover. A crashed aircraft was observed burning south-west of Rafah.

In between, on 8 January, the ILDF stated:

> In the afternoon, at approximately 1530, a flight of 12 aircraft flying in a northerly direction over Israeli territory was spotted north-east of Rafah. They were seen to be carrying wing bombs and were flying in battle formation, eight abreast and with four giving top cover. These planes were engaged by four Israeli fighters. One was seen to crash in flames while a second is claimed as probable. The remaining aircraft dispersed. All Israeli planes returned safely to base. Later, the burnt-out wreck of one RAF aircraft containing the remains of its pilot... was discovered near... Nirim.

The killed British pilot was David Crossley Tattersfield, a Squadron 213 Tempest pilot. The ILAF credited Schroeder with a kill.

A PILOT SHOULD KNOW WHAT TO LOOK FOR

1543–1608	3	0407	Lee	Tel Nof Dov Field
1545–1710	2	0401	Rubens	observation

Squadron 2 Commander Arie Rubens reported:

> Order was unclear: two Pipers to patrol Zeelim sector. Based on available information, I assumed that our tasking was to pinpoint an aircraft that was shot down west of Imara. I flew to Imara but saw nothing. I landed at Zeelim for further instructions but there was no one there to give [me instructions]. I took off and patrolled west and south of Zeelim; spotted only ILDF movements, especially between Zeelim and Nirim. Proceeded in direction of Rafah. A column of thick black smoke, rising to high altitude, was seen some two to three kilometers south-east of Rafah camp; dust clouds – perhaps moving vehicles – was seen east of this smoke... I did not notice any enemy movements. Returned to Zeelim and landed again to clarify objective of observation; met [Front D Air Liaison Officer] Freddy [Fredkins] who was unable to give me additional information... RTB. Orders must be more specific; a pilot should know what to look for!

END OF HOREV

1600–1910	1	1307)	Kaplan	Dov Field Beer Sheba Dov Field
1600–1930	1	1306	Ospovat	Dov Field Beer Sheba Dov Field
1800–1820	1	0412	Efrat/Lahat Porat	training
2000–2130	1	0602	Solarsh	Dov Field Ramat David Dov Field

HOREV's objective, the defeat of the EGDF in Israel, was not accomplished; the EGDF was not forced to retreat from the Gaza Strip and the Faluja Pocket was not eliminated. Still, HOREV was successful enough to force Egypt to seek a ceasefire and to agree to negotiation with Israel.

ILAFI issued, on 16 January 1949, a statistical analysis of ILAF offensive operations from 22 December 1948 until 7 January 1949. ILAFI indicated that during this timeframe, the ILAF dispatched 243 attack sorties, dropping 226 tons of bombs on 12 targets:

DAY	Faluja	Gaza	Khan Yunes	Rafah	El Arish	Dir Balah	Manshiya	other targets
0 (22)	3★Piper(342)		4★T-6(1,280)	3★C-47(3,927)	2★B-17(3,229)		1★Piper(144)	
1 (23)	4★T-6(1,600)	1★C-46(1,000)		2★C-47(3,200)				
2 (24)		2★B-17(2,940)	2★B-17(4,827)		1★Beauf(272)	3★T-6(1,089)		
		1★C-47(1,600)	3★T-6(1,200)					
3 (25)	1★C-47(1,690)			3★B-17(3,959)	3★B-17(5,390)			
	1★Piper(36)							
4 (26)	1★C-47(1,675)	1★C-46(2,600)		2★B-17(3,990)	2★B-17(3,136)			Abu Ageila 3★Piper(432)